MW00763637

Tim Baker is a former editor of *Tracks* and *Surfing Life* magazines, and former editorial director of Morrison Media Services. He is co-author of *Bustin' Down the Door*, the biography of '78 world surfing champion and ASP President Wayne 'Rabbit' Bartholomew (HarperCollins, 1996, now in its sixth print run). Tim holds a Bachelor of Journalism from the Royal Melbourne Institute of Technology, has completed a journalism cadetship at the Melbourne *Sun*, has won the Surfing Australia Hall of Fame Media Award and been shortlisted for the CUB Australian Sports Writing Awards. His work has appeared in *Rolling Stone*, the *Sydney Morning Herald*, *Inside Sport*, *Playboy*, *GQ*, the *Surfers Journal*, *Qantas: The Australian Way*, as well as surfing magazines around the world. He is currently a senior contributor to *Surfing World*, *Surfing Life*, the UK *Surfer's Path* and US *Surfing* and *Surfer* magazines. Now forty, he has worked in the media and surfing magazines for twenty years and has surfed and travelled throughout much of the world. He lives in Currumbin, Queensland, with his wife Kirsten and daughter Vivi, and is currently working on a surfing based novel.

WAVES
GREAT STORIES FROM THE SURF

Tim Baker
General Editor

Harper*Sports*
An imprint of HarperCollins*Publishers*

Harper*Sports*
An imprint of HarperCollins*Publishers*, Australia

First published in Australia in 2005
by HarperCollins*Publishers* Pty Limited
ABN 36 009 913 517
A member of the HarperCollins*Publishers* (Australia) Pty Limited Group
www.harpercollins.com.au

Introduction copyright © Tim Baker 2005
Compilation copyright © HarperCollins Publishers 2005
Copyright in the individual stories remains the property of the individual authors

Moral rights in the individual contributions remain the property of the authors
in accordance with the *Copyright Amendment (Moral Rights) Act 2000*.

This work is copyright.
Apart from any use as permitted under the *Copyright Act 1968*, no part may be reproduced,
copied, scanned, stored in a retrieval system, recorded or transmitted, in any form or by any
means, without the prior written permission of the publisher.

While efforts have been made to trace and acknowledge all copyright holders, in some cases
this has been unsuccessful. These copyright holders are very welcome to contact HarperCollins.

HarperCollins*Publishers*
25 Ryde Road, Pymble, Sydney NSW 2073, Australia
31 View Road, Glenfield, Auckland 10, New Zealand
77–85 Fulham Palace Road, London W6 8JB, United Kingdom
2 Bloor Street East, 20th Floor, Toronto, Ontario M4W 1A8, Canada
10 East 53rd Street, New York NY 10022, USA

National Library of Australia Cataloguing-in-Publication data:

Baker, Tim, 1965 –
   Waves: great stories from the surf.
   ISBN 0 7322 8330 2
   1. Short stories, Australian. 2. Surfing – Fiction.
   I. Baker, Tim, 1965 Jan. 16–.
A823.010832162

Cover image: A perfect wave fires its way down the reef at Backdoor on Oahu's North Shore.
Photographer: Sean Davey, 2001 (Surfpix)
Cover design by Katy Wright, HarperCollins Design Studio
Typeset in 11.5/16pt Goudy by Helen Beard, ECJ Australia Pty Ltd
Printed and bound in Australia by Griffin Press on 79gsm Bulky Paperback White

5 4 3 2 1   05 06 07 08

Contents

'In this country we may not have the ancient castles and cathedrals of Europe, the pyramids of Egypt, or temples of India, but at our great surf spots we have natural places of worship as magnificent as anything made by man's hand.'

Introduction

A brief history of surf writing

What do Captain James Cook, Herman Melville, Jack London, Mark Twain, Tom Wolfe, Sogyal Ringpoche, Timothy Leary and Tim Winton have in common?

They have all, at one time or another, applied their literary powers to the wonder of wave riding.

Perhaps I mention this to make myself feel better, to convince myself that having written about surfing for a living, for the last twenty years, is not evidence of some sort of emotional stuntedness — that this doesn't render me just another pop culture tragic, like some Surf Trek geek or custom car devotee, stuck in teenage obsessions.

Surfing is often portrayed as a realm of perpetual youth, something to grow out of, like acne or roller blading. But as I look about me in our increasingly crowded surf zones, I notice a greying and wrinkling of the lineups that speaks of a dedicated, lifelong love affair with the waves. It's one of the few things you can do with equal enthusiasm and passion at eight and eighty. There's a continual thread there, rare in our fast-forward world, a cultural continuum perfect for the passing on of stories. While the modern surf magazines might exist in a constant present, an endless fixation with the now — the newest star, the latest contest winner, the highest aerial, the next exotic surf discovery — I sense a steadily percolating interest in where we've come from, how we got here. The answers are in our shared stories, what we choose to pass on and record.

There is a long and colourful tradition of surf writing, of trying to evoke in words the mad, giddy, exhilarating beauty of wave riding — with wildly varying results. Perhaps only erotic literature walks quite the same fine line between the sublime and the ridiculous. And, like erotica, when the writing is seen as some desperate substitute for actually engaging in the physical activity, all that's aroused are the readers' suspicions.

The Polynesians, widely regarded as the first surfers, came up with the first surf stories, though these took the form of chants and myths and legends, passed on orally. They told of a deep and sophisticated view of surfing, central to their culture and reflecting an intimate, even sensual relationship with their environment:

> My board mounts the crest
> My loincloth flies in the spray of the sea
> I am like the *iwa* bird crying wildly
> As it soars so high above

Kahunas were called upon to raise the surf if it lay dormant too long, lashing the flat ocean with vines (*pohuehue*) to awaken it and leading the chanting:

> Arise, arise you great surfs from Kahiki,
> The powerful, curling waves, Arise with the *pohuehue*
> Well up, long raging surf

In *Traditions of Hawaii*, Hawaiian scholar Kepelino Keauokalani (1830–1878) explains there was great *hopupu* (excitement) as the surf season, Ikuwa, approached each November:

> It is a month of rough seas and high surf that lure men to the sea coast. For expert surfers going upland to farm, if part way up perhaps they look back and see the rollers combing the beach, will leave their work ... Then, hurrying away home, they will pick up the board and go. All thought of work is at an end, only that of sport is left. The wife may go hungry, the children, the whole family,

but the head of the house does not care. He is all for sport, that is his food. All day there is nothing but surfing. Many go out surfing as early as four in the morning — men, women, children. There is fine sport.

Perhaps under the influence of Christian missionaries, Keauokalani seems to have attached some deep moral failing to this condition: 'From innocent pleasures they turn to evil pleasures; so it goes.'

The missionaries are widely blamed for almost wiping out surfing in Hawaii in the 1800s, as a heathen pastime. But at least one, a Rev. Henry T. Cheever (In *Life of the Sandwich Islands*, 1851) was enthusiastic about surfing and its health-giving benefits:

> The sport is so attractive and full of wild excitement to Hawaiians, and withal so healthful, that I cannot but hope it will be many years before civilization shall look it out of countenance, or make it disreputable to indulge in this manly though dangerous exercise ... The missionaries at these islands, and foreigners generally, are greatly at fault in that they do not avail themselves more of this easy and unequalled means of retaining health, or of restoring it when enfeebled.

Early European explorers were inevitably awed by the sight of surfing and moved to poetic attempts to describe the marvel. Captain James Cook was clearly entranced by the spectacle of canoe surfing when he first came upon it in Tahiti in 1777, and wrote (in *Cook's Voyages* Vol. II Chapter IX): 'Neither are they (the Tahitians) strangers to the soothing effects produced by particular sorts of motion, which in some cases seem to allay any pertubation of the mind with as much success as music . . .' He went on to describe a man busily catching waves, oblivious to the presence of the European ship and sailors nearby. 'I could not help concluding that this man felt the most supreme pleasure while he was driven on so fast and so smoothly by the sea . . .'

Mark Twain was one of the first surf chroniclers to actually try his hand at surfboard riding as related graphically in a chapter titled 'Native Surf Bathing' in his 1866 book, *Roughing It*:

I tried surf bathing once, subsequently, but made a failure of it. I got the board placed right, and at the right moment, too; but missed the connection myself. The board struck the shore in three quarters of a second, without any cargo, and I struck the bottom about the same time, with a couple of barrels of water in me. None but natives ever master the art of surf-bathing thoroughly.

Jack London visited Hawaii on board the *Snark* in 1907 and wrote of the surfer as a god:

Where but the moment before was only the wide desolation and invincible roar, is now a man, erect, full-statured, not struggling frantically in that wild movement, not buried and crushed and buffeted by those mighty monsters, but standing above them all, calm and superb, poised on the giddy summit, his feet buried in the churning foam, the salt smoke rising to his knee, and all the rest of him in the free air and flashing sunlight, and he is flying through the air, flying forward, flying fast as the surge on which he stands. He is a Mercury, a brown Mercury. His heels are winged, and in them is the swiftness of the sea . . .

Of course, the story of Australian surfing, and surf writing, begins with the famous visit and demonstration by the champion Hawaiian swimmer, Duke Kahanamoku, in Sydney in 1914. Or does it? Surf bathing, or body surfing, was popular at many coastal centres well before the Duke's visit. In a 1912 publication, 'Sport and Pastime in Australia,' author Gordon Inglis included a chapter, 'The Joy of Surf', in which he writes:

An old-established rowing club in Sydney disbanded a little while back, and a friend communicating the intelligence, wrote, 'The main cause was the depletion in the ranks — they all surf.' . . . No recreation has taken such a hold upon the community, nor could progress have been more rapid. At the beginning of the twentieth century surf bathing in Australia was practically unknown. Even in 1903 the number of devotees was very small, and there were many annoying restrictions governing the pastime. It proved a difficult matter to convince some municipal potentates that the ardent supporters of surfing were not animated by unworthy intent.

Body surfers could be found all up and down the east coast, Inglis reported. He even foreshadowed the current companion pastime of golf among today's wealthy pro surfers, and the surf-inspired boom in coastal real estate:

Wherever it be you will find a crowd of happy sun-worshippers, revelling in the delights of shooting the breakers, to be followed by the healthy and invigorating sun bath. The South Coast now boasts of many golf clubs. To laze away the holiday hours with surfing and golf in plenty, both in ideal surroundings — he a selfish fellow who asks for more . . . Moreover, it has become recognized that the value of land in the vicinity of the most attractive bathing spots has been enormously increased. Allotments, that a dozen years ago would not have aroused a vestige of interest, have changed hands at a high figure. The attitude of the local authority is refreshingly altered, and the leading beaches are now properly equipped with dressing-room accommodation, etc. Thus has one of the healthiest pastimes come to its own.

Though there were some surfboards in Australia prior to the Duke's visit (imported from Hawaii or copied from Hawaiian boards), the arrival of the renowned swimmer and wave rider was keenly anticipated to help show the locals how it was done. In 1914, just prior to the great man's visit, Cecil Healy wrote with impressive prescience about the impact the Duke's display here might have:

> Kahanamoku is a wonderfully dextrous performer on the surfboard, an instrument of pleasure that Australians have so far been unsuccessful in handling to any degree. Reports have been brought back from overseas of his acrobatic feats executed while dashing shorewards at great speeds, but one doubts the possibility of Duke, or anyone else, duplicating such feats in Australian surf. Still, if he should give one of his rare exhibitions for our edification, be sure it will create a keen desire on the part of our ambitious shooters to emulate his deeds, and it goes without saying that his movements will be watched intently. Personally, I am convinced that the natural amphibious attitude of the Australians will enable one or another to unravel the knack.

Reports on the Duke's exhibitions in Sydney were unanimous in their enthusiasm:

WONDERFUL SURF RIDING

KAHANAMOKU ON THE BOARD

A THRILLING SPECTACLE

So the Sydney *Sun* trumpeted on 24 December 1914, above a rapturous account by W.F. Corbett:

One could hear, in the imagination, the roars of applause with which thousands of Australians might have greeted Kahanamoku's display at Freshwater, Manly, this morning, had the fact that it was to take place been made public. As it was there were only a few pressmen, some members of the New South Wales Amateur Swimming Association, and the casual Freshwater bathers present . . .

This finely-built Hawaiian, with his powerful frame showing elastic muscles, as better and more enduring than those of a knotty nature, caught the breaker he wanted, and paddling along for a while rose to one knee first, then became gradually erect and reached the crest to shoot forward with astonishing speed and marvellous balance . . . The ease and grace of his shooting might be equalled, but it certainly could not be excelled. As showing how much second nature it was to him, Kahanamoku stood on his head a couple of times, and even turned his back to the direction in which he was going, and posed. Lying flat on the board, the Hawaiian caused it to describe a half-circle or turn completely round without spoiling the shoot.

Such was the effect of the Duke's visit that, by 1917, Australia had its first surfing periodical, the *Surf*, published as a small newspaper that survived for twenty issues into 1918. According to its masthead, the *Surf*'s objective was 'The development and protection of our beaches', apparently seeing no conflict between these twin goals. It was probably the first magazine in the world devoted to surfing and the beach. Editor Con Drew included horse racing and swimming results, women's fashion and social events, and witty captions alongside photos, mainly of women at play in the surf.

'The sight of a surfboard to Frank Foran is as sweet as the smell of grease paint to an actor,' read one caption.

'Bill Craven's surfboard shot him so high the other day that he's only just come down. Oh girls! Supposing he hadn't,' exclaimed another caption.

The initial response seems to have been enthusiastic.

'Last Friday we printed 5000 copies, and by Saturday night we'd sold clean out,' the editor claimed in the second issue.

The war years may have stifled the growth of surfing and there appear to have been few further attempts at Australian surf publishing until the great boom period of the late '50s and '60s. Prior to this period, surfboard riding in Australia was largely absorbed into the established surf life-saving culture.

An illustrated surf guide was produced in Sydney in 1931. *Surf: All About It* boldly declared: '*Surf* contains the condensed knowledge and wisdom of the surf-aces for EVERYBODY to read. You can become a surf-ace as soon as you like — shoot the breakers, if you want to, as expertly as the brownest champion of them all.'

Australian surfing changed forever with the arrival of a US surf team in 1956, to coincide with the Melbourne Olympics. They put on surfing displays at Torquay in Victoria and at Manly and Avalon in Sydney on their new, shorter and lighter Malibu boards and blew the minds of Australian surfers with their control and deft manoeuvres. Among the wide-eyed spectators at Manly was a young Bernard 'Midget' Farrelly, who would later become Australia's first men's world champion at that same beach, in 1964.

The interceding eight years were a time of rapid change and growth in Australian surfing. Magazines sprang up from 1961 — first the shortlived *Australian Surfer*, and *Surfabout*, and then *Surfing World*, which seemed to strike the right chord and endures today.

In a retrospective article in *SW* in 1972, the magazine's founder Bob Evans, also a keen surf film-maker, recalled the radical changes of the '60s. The catalyst, he says, was the release of the movie 'Gidget,' and 'an awakening interest overnight became a raging psychedelic giant.' The success of 'Gidget' made surfing ripe for commercial exploitation, while the image of the thrill-chasing, anti-establishment surfer set off alarm bells in the older generation. 'Out of the associated publicity emerged a word which was publicly accepted as the noun relative to the species — SURFIE,' wrote Evans.

Right on cue, in 1966, one of the first so-called 'surfsploitation' paperback novels, *Surfie*, appeared, written by Roger Carr. The coverline blared: 'Chuck was the craziest surfie,

chasing the perfect wave or the perfect femlin [female surfer] —
sometimes he caught both.'

This was quite a shift. Much of the earlier Australian surf
writing had been strictly practical and instructional in nature,
tutoring in technique and relating new surf discoveries. In the
'60s there was John Bloomfield's *Know-how in the Surf* and Jack
Pollard's, *The Australian Surfrider*, both now keenly sought by
collectors. Geoff Carter produced perhaps the first Australian
surf location guide, *Surf Beaches of Australia's East Coast*, in a
white leatherette hard cover.

Surf writing of the time seems quite proper, quaint even,
through the telescope of time. But in the late '60s, almost
overnight, it was as if someone had put something in the water
— and perhaps they had — as surf writing grew increasingly
esoteric, mimicking free-form beat poetry or improvised jazz in
rambling stream of consciousness raves, some profound, some
indecipherable. Surfers were riding waves in a whole new way, on
radically shortened equipment, and writers of the day struggled
to convey these new surfing sensations.

Legendary surfer/shaper Bob MacTavish cut loose in a series
of landmark articles in *Surf International* in 1967, with titles like
'Ladies and Gentlemen and Children of the Sun,' extolling
surfers to, 'stroll, run, leap, laugh in gardens of crystal motion
and sun and reality.'

Tracks magazine arrived on the scene in 1970, with a photo of
the Newcastle steelworks inexplicably on the cover, giving a
platform for deep eco-raves, vegetarian cooking columns,

instructions on building a tree house, and protests against sand mining. In the '70s, surf writing seemed to oscillate between this counter-culture consciousness and Aussie sporting yobboism.

Bill Bennett proved feminism had yet to reach Australian surfing in a little essay entitled 'Surf Ladies', observing, 'They do make pretty little spectators don't they?' Having someone to cook, do the laundry and wash the dishes were just some of the advantages he highlighted in having a female surf companion.

Meanwhile, a more enlightened Laurie McGinness was asking the big questions: 'Would a 360-degree arc on the face be more spiritually rewarding than kissing Lotus Feet of the Buddha in the Highest State of Transcendental Meditation?'

Surf poetry spread like lantana, with lavish evocations of 'turquoise energy', 'crystalline vortexes' and 'pressurised liquid rodeos', amid photo spreads of pandanus trees, topless girls, albatross in flight, driftwood and old farmhouses.

Eerily accurate prophecies abound in old surfing magazines. One of Australia's great surfing pioneers, and Australian board champion from 1926 to 1928, C.J. 'Snowy' McAlister, wrote a letter to *Sea Notes* magazine in 1978, on the recent innovation of jet skis, with uncanny foresight. Snowy had just witnessed Narrabeen surfer Col Smith riding large waves on one of the new Kawasaki two-stroke jet skis and marvelled at his 'great skill' and 'long tube rides' but he also worried about this motorised 'intrusion into our surfing domain'. In his wisdom, Snowy imagined a future where the new equipment would be used to 'zoom out seawards and tackle some of the bombora surfs when working off our beaches. What a sight we are in for.' Twenty years later, as predicted, surfers began using jet skis to 'tow-in' to huge previously unrideable outer reef waves.

In the late '70s Phil Jarratt at *Tracks* set the template for the great Aussie tradition of merciless piss-taking — roasting the world's first pro surf team, the Bronzed Aussies, and fuelling surfing's great cultural debate of the age: is surfing sport or art? Jarratt's description of his personal sporting nirvana — watching the Stubbies Classic surf contest, from a Burleigh Heads highrise apartment balcony, swivelling his head 180 degrees to watch the Test cricket on the TV, while drinking beer — remains a classic of the genre.

Nick Carroll and Derek Hynd weighed in in the early '80s, setting a new standard as both accomplished competitive surfers and talented writers. Hynd penned many a shadowy essay of esoteric musings, in apparent attempts to excorcise surfing's collective demons. And Carroll's annual, intimately involved Hawaiian reports transported the reader to the throbbing lineups of the North Shore with stunning intensity.

The techniques of the so-called new journalism — the styles of Tom Wolfe and Hunter S. Thompson, with the writer as a dynamic and often deranged participant in events — were warmly embraced by the surf media. 'Fear and Loathing' headlines abounded, and the stereotype of the dishevelled surf reporter, skulking about the well-lubricated hospitality tents of major pro contests, was deservedly forged.

For all this, and though they may never qualify as high literature, surfing magazines remain a rare bastion of free expression. Pick up a modern surf magazine and you are likely to find anarchy, misogyny, hedonism, and materialism alongside rose-tinted, soulful yearnings for the simpler days of yesteryear and deep, new age enviro-rants. You will find abundant evidence of surfers' obsessions with their genitals, cars, surfboards, waves, lovers and mind-altering substances, as well as notions of nationhood, cultural identity, elite athleticism, proud tribalism, mysticism and a deep connection to their environment.

Today, surf writing comes in all hues and flavours, as this collection attests. From rough justice on the streets of Maroubra to questions about the very origins of wave riding. From epiphanies in the midst of Hawaiian inter-island paddling, to hi-tech media expeditions to remotest Indonesia, to the beautiful surfing evocations of, perhaps, Australia's greatest living novelist, Tim Winton. Jack Finlay calls surfing 'a moveable feast' in his essay, 'Wind on the Water,' and that it is — spiced with exotic new tastes in its many and varied settings.

What has become blindingly obvious from this quick trawl through history is that surfing has always stirred deep passions in its observers and participants. The spectacle of humans harnessing and riding this pure, natural energy form speaks to some deep yearning in us for a more daring, graceful and joyful way of being. Surfers have adventures, leave the land, paddle out to sea, and make play at the ragged edges of vast oceans. They are held under water to the limits of their lungs' endurance. They confront sharks and other marine life. They are dashed across reefs in remote and exotic locations. They find euphoric sport in the fleeting death throes of ocean pulses that have travelled across the world. And they return to land somehow changed, shaped and moulded by the watery elements that so enthral them.

I hope you enjoy, even find inspiration in, this collection. Go surfing. Go tell someone about it. There — you just made a surf story. To trade waves with a few friends at any one of the beautiful surf locations around our coastline, and afterwards to share food, drink, laughter and stories, is surely one of life's 'supreme pleasures', as Captain Cook would say. Or, as Gordon Inglis put it back in 1912, 'he a selfish fellow who asks for more.'

But don't forget that golden rule: if you are talking or writing about surfing more than you're doing it, maybe you should be doing more surfing.

And with that, I think I'll pop off and take my own advice . . .

Tim Baker
Currumbin, Queensland, November 2005

1

HEROES AND VILLAINS

Where you catch your first wave leaves an imprint that can last a lifetime

Phil Jarratt

When I started high school in February 1964 I had been surfing for just over a year and it had yet to take over my life, but all that was about to change very quickly.

Corrimal High School was a nondescript red brick postwar nightmare — no form, no function — wedged between the escarpment and the sea towards the northern end of the NSW south coast. Its least appealing feature was the asphalt quadrangle adjacent to the main building, a no-man's-land with prison-style bench seating around its perimeter, too hot in summer, too cold in winter. Its most appealing feature was its proximity to East Corrimal beach, a pleasant enough stretch of sand hemmed in by high dunes and divided by a creek mouth which kept the sand banks relatively stable.

By the most direct route, the beach we called 'Brandies' (for no apparent reason) was about half a kilometre away — a five-minute walk or a two-minute cruise on a pushie. But because the direct route went past the front door of the Starlings (he the English and history master, she the school librarian) it was necessary during school hours to use a more circuitous route, through the colourful migrant neighbourhood that soon became my beat, and my boardstore.

The guys from the 'hood surfed before school all year round, and would drip saltwater from their noses as they described the epic early session you'd missed. I couldn't do earlies, for two very good reasons: I wasn't allowed and I didn't have a board. In my first months of high school I borrowed boards from guys called Piet and Bruno and Jurek, incredibly heavy Norm Caseys or Jackson & Cansdells with reverse skegs abutting the tailblock. I would sit at the tide line and wait for the surf to blow out so I could beg a few waves from the incoming surfers.

I thus learnt to surf on a variety of equipment totally unsuited to my lightweight prepubescent frame, and the legacy of this unfortunate start may be lingering in certain stylistic deficiencies even today, but let's not torture ourselves with what might have been. And in any case my boardless condition sometimes resulted in unlikely tuition. One blown-out midweek afternoon the great Bobby Brown lent me his Jacko and actually waded out with me and showed me how to stand on the deck and push through the soup — a totally cool move which became my *pièce de résistance*, way before I could turn both ways.

I was promised a surfboard to commemorate my becoming a teenager in July, so the search began to find one within the allocated ten quid. With the help of the Brothers Olejniczak, Franco-Polish Aussies who had become my best buds at the beach, I settled on a Barry Bennett nine-four with a highly suspect grey–purple pigment job. Pat O, later to become a minor manufacturer himself, checked it over and pronounced it not waterlogged, so Dad forked out eight pounds ten shillings and the thing was mine!

We lived in WASP country on the side of the mountain overlooking the coast, the metropolis of Wollongong and, yes, the largest smokestack in the southern hemisphere in far-off Port Kembla. This was cool for Mum and Dad, but for me it was a freakin' long walk with 30 kilos of surfboard on a towel on my head. I yearned to be in Action Central, the beachside 'hood where refugees from the war in Europe had made a new life in brightly painted fibro bungalows and were only beginning to come to terms with their peroxide-haired outlaw teenage sons. Dad made me a board carrier from pieces of bike frame he found in his cycle shop, but I used it only rarely before I was awarded (for gromly persistence, slight surfing improvement, and the exhibition of definite delinquent tendencies) membership of Dino's Shed.

Membership of Dino's Shed was the shit in the 'hood of East Corrimal in '64, I can tell you. It not only meant that you could deposit your stick there, securely stored, about 200 metres from the beach; it meant that you were part of the cool crew, that you could park your towel and wax on the Team Dune, join in the dirty jokes (even if you didn't understand them) and, on surfless afternoons, cruise along the beach to the Towradgi Baths in a pack, looking for trouble. Membership of Dino's Shed also helped (but this was not automatic) with admission to the parties at Dino's Shack, a tin and brush affair that lasted a couple of summers in the dunes before the cops got wise to it.

Dino's Shed was a meeting point; Dino's Shack was a mating point. In the tradition of the best surf cultures in the world, many an innocence was lost by the glow of Dino's bonfire, surrounded by surfboards and beer bottles, with coarse sand doing serious damage to your privates.

Dino himself was a charismatic blond-haired goofyfoot, a natural leader who retained a sense of inner self and quiet decorum, despite the appalling behaviour of his gang. Dino went to the war and came back a wild-eyed recluse, but in '64 and '65, on our beach, he was the man.

At the beginning of the summer of '64–65, a big, beefy bozo of a guy — half surfer, half clubbie — opened a surf shop next to Col Mason's barber shop adjacent to the main school gate. It was called the Corrimal Surf Hut and the owner was Darrell Eastlake. When I worked with Big Daz on Channel Nine many, many years later, I used to kid him about what a chick magnet he was back then. Well, he did OK, I'm sure, but it was the rattan and coconut palm atmosphere of the little shop that appealed to all of us. On flat afternoons, you could hang out and stroke the immaculate glass jobs of the latest Dillons, Jackos and Caseys, while checking the Little Pattie lookalikes from third form. Daz always had the latest *Surfers* and *Peterson's Surf Guide* mags from California, which was the centre of the universe, and he seemed to be on first-name terms with anyone who mattered, like Midget Farrelly or Bob Pike.

Within months he had founded the Corrimal Boardriders Club, which I joined briefly before deserting for the rival Bellambi Boardriders. Darrell was cool and fun and, I'm sure, a huge worry to the fathers of young girls with salt in their hair and lust in their hearts.

The best surfer in our school was Kevin Parkinson, who was in 3F the year I was in 1A. The F class was as low as you could go short of 'Special Learning Difficulties', and it was full of surfers, of course. The guys in the F class didn't give a rat's arse. They were getting the hell out of school as soon as they were legal at fourteen years and ten months, straight into a good-paying job in the coal mine and plenty of time to surf.

The 3F guys were cool, but Kevin was the coolest of the cool. He was quite short but stockily built and he kind of swaggered. He had a huge wave of unruly brown hair and a permanently curled bottom lip. If he wasn't surfing, he was being one of the guys who smoked cigarettes behind the toilet block at lunch time. In fact one of the coolest things I ever saw him do was this:

at Bellambi on a four-foot day he lit a ciggie, picked up his board and cruised along the baths' wall, jumped off and knee-paddled into the lineup, then took off on a wave, casually walked to the nose and draped ten while he ashed his cigarette onto the face and blew smoke rings. Sitting in front of the toilet block, out of the southerly, our gallery of groms went wild.

At the weekend Parko hung out with a Towradgi-based crew led by Troy Williams, who was older and had a car. During the week at school he hung out with Brian 'Apey' McLeod. Sensitively nicknamed by his peers for a gait caused by childhood polio, Apey actually used his affliction to advantage in the surf, using his stump as a drop-knee pivot. Parko and Apey were the first guys in the school to wear wide-leg Lee jeans and Keds sneakers. In 1A we were in awe.

When the wind blew offshore and the beachies were working, the various tribes congregated at their own home breaks, but when the southerly swells hit, there was a huge gathering in the old dirt (often mud) car park at Bellambi. Sandon was a better wave, but Bellambi had a San Onofre feel to it — campfires and parties after dark, girls disappearing into panel vans. Ken Middleton, Mick Carabine and John Skipp would show up from Wollongong, Paul 'Dirtyface' Brooks and his crew from Port Kembla, John Batcheldore and Albert Fox from Warilla . . . and best of all, Bobby Brown and the other heroes from Cronulla. Gary Birsdall was always one, a quiet, authoritative presence in and out of the surf.

At the end of the summer of '64–65, as I moved up to 2A and Parko left school to surf and help his mum make boardshorts, a guy at our beach watched me surf one afternoon and told me conspiratorially, 'What you need is a bigger board, to straighten out your surfing.' He led me to his Mini Cooper and took an apple green Norm Casey nine-eight off the roof. The board was very, um, bright, virtually ding-free and boasted one of the newfangled moulded plastic pintail fins. He let me ride it. I couldn't turn it but I could see exactly what he meant — set your line at the takeoff, don't flap around and don't deviate. I bought the board with my savings from the paper run, and set back my progress by at least a year.

For the next five years, until I left the 'Gong forever in January 1970, East Corrimal and Bellambi were the centre of my existence. The scene of surfing PBs (a Hakman-style cheater five manoeuvre to actually win a heat in a club comp comes to mind, as such rarities do), great personal tragedies (Peter Tweedle and I both copping a rail in the mush and knocking out our front teeth on the same day), sexual awakenings and the formulation of lasting friendships, our home beaches, like anyone's, were almost mythological places in the heart.

I sometimes go back to visit family, and usually try to get wet. East Corrimal is still much the same, although I'm sure the banks were better back in my day! Bellambi is profoundly depressing. Not only have safe-harbour extensions cut off the swell, but the old track through the rifle range has been replaced by an asphalt jungle peopled by trailer trash who have come to rest. You can almost feel the despair as you drive past the cul-de-sacs of neglected cottages and overgrown lawns.

If I was starting to surf today, I would probably try to do it somewhere else. But you don't get to choose the location of your gromhood, and if it disappears along with so many members of the cast — blown away by the pressures of the times — then all you can do is treasure your memories, and paddle out squinting so much that the goatboater taking off in front of you might even be Parko running to the nose, blowing smoke rings defiantly in the air.

First published in *Pacific Longboarder*, 2002.

2

WHEN WORLDS COLLIDE

Kelly Slater and friends take surfing cross-cultural exchange to new and surreal heights in remotest Indonesia

Tim Baker

Indies Trader skipper Martin Daly recently went for a surf by sea plane. Left his home in Jakarta, flew to Panaitan Island, West Java, surfed overhead One Palm Point with two other guys for a couple of hours, and was back home in time for lunch.

'I was sitting in the pub and my boardies were still wet,' Martin laughs, as if he can't quite believe the absurdity of it. The kind of surf mission that once required weeks of preparation and planning by boat is now a quick dip in your lunch break. This kind of thing is Martin's gig these days — pulling off the most audacious surf missions at the drop of a hat, like a kid playing with his battleships in the bath.

Ten years ago, Martin was a salvage diver who just happened to stumble upon some of the greatest undiscovered surf spots in the world in his travels through South East Asia. Today he commands a fleet of three of the plushest, best-equipped surf charter boats in the business — *Indies Trader I, II* and *III* — and commands princely sums from a well-heeled clientele of surf stars, surf industry heavyweights, and independently wealthy old surf-dogs and trust-fund kids.

But this latest venture was something else altogether. Two boats (*Indies Trader I* and *II*), seven surfers, two jet skis, five cameramen, an internet technician and . . . me. I found out I was going two days before I flew out, on an expedition billed as 'Kelly Slater — Outside the Boundaries', which sounded to me like something you got into trouble for at school, when you nicked off at lunch time to smoke ciggies.

And so, there I was, winging my way to some Indian Ocean outpost before I'd even had time to consider what kind of surf mission required the presence of Kelly Slater, Tom Carroll and big-wave nutters Ross Clarke-Jones, Peter Mel and Dave Kalama. A couple of hot groms — Ry Craike, from Western Australia, and Dylan Graves from Puerto Rico — were chucked in at the last minute to round out the mix.

'I pulled this whole thing together on Wednesday,' Martin laughed, merrily, as he collected us from the steamy Third World airport. It was now Saturday.

Over tall glasses of cold draught beer in the hotel bar — as Martin laid out the whole crazy plan and his recent adventures (like the seaplane biz) — it hit me. Martin was Scotty, from the old 'Thunderbirds' TV show, with its fleet of space age aircraft ready to rush to any international calamity. Like Scotty, Martin presided over his fleet of charter boats, at the ready for any eventuality, consulting charts and swell maps, and despatching his crews to the furthest reaches of the surfable world at a moment's notice. 'The new boat can go from Padang to Durban on one tank of fuel,' he boasted. I could almost picture him in his office, a red blip flashing in some far-flung corner of the Indian Ocean on a wall-size map of the world, a portrait of one of his skippers rotating on the wall, as he sternly informed them: 'Virgil, this is Scotty, we got a hot one for you.'

Except Virgil in this case was Albert, a curly, flame-haired, fortyish, nuggety natural footer from Shell Harbour, who'd been plying these waters since 1984, and was none too excited about ferrying a boatful of pro surfers and media personnel to his beloved secret spots. 'If any of you do anything to identify any of these places, I will personally come after you,' he growled, when we first gathered on the *Indies Trader I*. 'A lot of crew have done it tough for a lot of years to get to these places,' he told us coldly. He had a point.

Martin even had his own 'Brains', a shrewd mastermind who took care of onland logistics. Julian was a pale-skinned, forty-something, classic expat, worn into submission by the endless lessons in patience and absurdity such Third World locales provide in bulk. 'Julian knows more about this place than any white man alive,' Martin told me. Julian had worked for the New Zealand Government, overseeing the administration of foreign aid here, then the World Bank, and most recently the United Nations, before he'd hit the wall. 'It drives you crazy watching millions of dollars just disappear into the system,' Julian explained. He obviously knew his way round this place.

So, the next morning, as we crammed bodies, boards and baggage into our dodgy little chartered cargo plane, I was a tad concerned when Julian asked Martin anxiously why there was a red light flashing on the pilot's control panel. With nothing separating us from the cockpit, Julian went forward and consulted with the pilots to see whether they'd checked the oil recently. Perhaps someone's door wasn't shut properly, I wondered hopefully. Julian seemed satisfied and settled back into his seat. Airline staff distributed those quaint little cardboard boxes of Unidentified Fried Objects and hurried off the plane, as the propellers spluttered to life and we lurched off down the runway. Anyhow, I reassured myself, how much trouble could you get into with such impressive safety provisions as the small metal first-aid kit and the pickaxe I saw bolted to the wall?

The pungent smell of *durian*, a favourite local fruit that smells like someone with an unwell bottom, hung heavily in the air as I braced myself for a rugged takeoff — eyes closed, deep breathing. Then, suddenly, I opened my eyes and peered out the window to see the ground hastily disappearing into the distance beneath us. Our plane was a Casa — a Spanish-designed but locally built piece of aeronautical history. It was made for mountainous terrain, where it can take off and land on as little as 800 metres of runway, Julian explained expertly. We were up, up and away before I had time to even get scared.

The main talking point en route seemed to be the recent trip of mighty legends Darrick Doerner, Gerry Lopez and Al Byrne, who had scored 15 feet, top-to-bottom barrelling rights in this vicinity. Towed in by jet ski, Martin reckoned, there was no way out of the things until you popped out of the barrel a couple of hundred metres down the reef. Lopez scored one such hair-raising tube on his backhand and paddled back to the boat, grateful to still be alive. Doerner, or 'Double D' as his mates call him, was moved to tears by the sheer intensity of the experience, recounting it later. While the others had gone home to wives and families and jobs and normal lives, Darrick couldn't quite bring himself to go and had set up camp on the *Indies III* as a kind of volunteer lifeguard for Martin's well-to-do clientele.

Surfers and cameramen had been flown in at a few days' notice to take part in the great Slater-fest — a rare opportunity to view the six-time world champion in action, like a sighting of a rare and exotic bird. Kelly himself arrived at this dusty port riding on the roof of a dilapidated old minibus with his boardbags and a couple of locals, like any other carefree Third World traveller. It was an image that seemed to speak volumes for his current frame of mind — to climb out of the suffocating confines of his usual space, to feel the wind in his hair, to travel as a simple man, stripped bare. Or maybe I'm reading too much into it . . .

Regardless, our crew assembled after some delay and set about stowing boards and claiming bunks. I wandered into the little town nearby and had a haircut from a local lady in a busy general store, while a pack of kids swarmed around our feet, customers came and went, and a strange Japanese superhero show like 'Power Rangers' flickered on the TV in the corner. A magnificent poster on the wall illustrated fifty or so men's hairstyles you could choose from — all apparent variations on enormous James Brown bouffants. Thankfully, I escaped with a neat short back and sides. Next door we ate lunch: local style fish, rice and vegies for about four bucks for three of us. Kids rode battered boards at a tiny sandpoint out front, and a busker strummed a homemade ukelele on the street corner. Grand temples of at least three major religions — Christian, Hindu and Islamic — dominated the small town.

An armed troop of soldiers turned up at the dock to watch over our departure, fresh-faced boys really, in crisp uniforms with high-powered rifles slung over shoulders as flippantly as schoolbags. We loaded up and buggered the hell off. With a swell already hitting, we had a night's motoring before we reached surf. Our cook, Mick, reckoned he'd never seen the little point in town break before. There had to be waves out there.

The skipper of *Indies II* was Jody Perry, who came third in the very first Pro Junior back in '77, which was won by Tom Carroll, and here they were reunited in rather different circumstances. Jody still rips and has built his life around boats, the sea and surfing perfect waves well off the beaten track. You wonder if, with a few twists of fate, their roles might have been reversed and Jody might have been the surf star and Tom the salty sea-dog skipper.

First stop was a six- to eight-foot Sunset-like right-hander that looked kind of weird, with big rearing peaks outside and lumpy fat sections in the middle, but some screaming barrels on the inside. There was a crude little camp on land but no one surfing and our boys were soon into it. Tom was amazing. At nearly forty and with arthroscopic knee surgery eight weeks before, he was squeaking under lips and pulling into gaping barrels like it was Sunset in the mid-80s and there was a world title on the line. Kelly stood tall and proud in the biggest, cleanest barrel rides of the day. Ross, of course, was right at home in this sort of stuff, as was big Petey Mel, freefalling out of lips and gouging faces like it was a playful beachbreak. Dave Kalama took out his longboard and stroked into big swells way outside and backdoored the peak. And the groms had a good dig too. Dylan, fifteen but looking about ten, from Puerto Rico, is the current NSSA east coast explorer boys champ. The waves were about four times overhead and he was on a five-foot-seven doing grabrail cutties. 'I think I need bigger fins or something,' he suggested afterwards — 'something' being perhaps an extra foot or two of surfboard and 40 kilos more bodyweight. He'd found out he was coming two days before the trip, when he was in California for a comp, and his mum had Fed-Exed his boards to him.

Ry Craike, a charger, from Kalbarri, who started life as a natural foot until his dad told him he should be a goofy, so he could surf the famed local left-hand reef on his forehand. Since then he's never looked back. His dad's an abalone diver and drags him out to Western Australia's offshore reefs and islands at every opportunity, towing him into serious open ocean waves behind a jet ski. Nothing seemed to faze him.

There were a bunch of Pommies, a few Spaniards and the inevitable Aussies staying on land, all paying 50 cents a night for their simple beachfront cabins, and anywhere from $2 to $6 a day for three meals. It took four days to get here overland — by bus, public ferry and finally rickety local fishing boats. There was malaria and dengue fever and no hospital for hundreds of miles. A bloke broke his back the week before, and a helicopter flew in to carry him out. Luckily, he had medivac travel insurance — don't leave home without it. One fella, Don, scored the quinella when he contracted malaria and dengue fever during a four-month stay last year, but he was back for another four months this year. He'd cracked his ribs already this trip and retreated to civilisation for a few weeks to convalesce, then came back for the rest of the season. 'What do they do about girls?' Kelly wanted to know. 'I'd go crazy.'

All this hardship and you'd think a bunch of highly paid pro surfers turning up in a couple of luxury charter boats, with a swag of cameramen in tow, might piss the occupants off. Not a bit of it. The lads on land couldn't have been more happy to see us.

'It's not every day you get to see surfing like this,' one of them reckoned, gallantly giving up his verandah for one of our cameramen to shoot from all day.

While the surf stars made fascinating viewing, some of the characters bunkered down in this surfing Gilligan's Island (without the girls) were just as intriguing. The Spaniards charged hard and got some insane barrels, and the Poms did themselves proud too. One new arrival, a late-thirties Aussie fellow, got chatting to me, out in the lineup one morning, like an old friend. Just a regular working family man doing the overland thing to brush off the cobwebs. 'I took a month off. I had to do it, I hadn't been away for three years. If I didn't do it now, I never would,' he reasoned, convincingly. 'Even the missus was keen for me to get away.' He looked a bit short of peak condition, carrying a few extra pounds, a bit red in the face, not lean and tanned like an everyday surfer — someone who'd been working more than surfing. The next thing, he's stroking into this rearing A-frame, right on the apex of the peak, and I wonder if he's up to it. He throws himself over the ledge, late and critical, driving down the face confidently and into a strong sure-footed bottom turn around a mountain of whitewater and off down the line, no problem.

In that moment, I felt like I'd witnessed the rebirth of a surfer, eyes wide, cheeks puffed, body straining, but all the old instincts sharp and intact. In years to come, I'd wager, he'll look back on that trip as a pivotal point in his life, the fork in the road where he chose to remain a surfer rather than tip over into the abyss of suburban, nine-to-five oblivion.

We'd caught the tail end of a swell, but it soon began to drop. There is some danger in pronouncing a trip a Serious Tow-in Mission. It happened last time they tried it on the Crossing — loaded up with big wave he-men and jet skis and tow boards and tow ropes and the whole nine yards, somewhere in the South Pacific last year. Of course — no swell. Tom was on to it as soon as he saw this billed as a Tow trip. 'Don't call it a tow trip,' he warned, understanding full well the inescapable laws of nature ready to doom such a venture. Ever gone out at night with casual sex foremost in your mind? Go on, admit it. Ever noticed that, if you are responsible enough to pack condoms, they seem to send out an invisible signal from your coin pocket or wallet, on a special frequency only women can detect, that reveals you as a desperate, lecherous, heat-seeking missile? Packing connies almost guarantees you a lonely night. Same with jet skis, tow boards and big wave heroes. Pack them, and the swell is sure to evaporate. Quikkie reckons the best waves on the whole Crossing have been the 'no hero' trips, where it's all the forty- or fifty-something senior execs or hapless office staff, suddenly stroking for their lives in huge Hawaiian-style surf, without a surf star or camera to be found.

Expectations, you see, kill possibilities. When you have a preconceived notion of what a trip, or a night out or a run down the coast should be to qualify as a success, you kill the magic of spontaneity, unforeseen new options and the wonder of the moment.

With all this pulsing testosterone, finely tuned tow boards and highly powered jet skis on board, and no life-threatening waves, something had to give.

'Things explode out on boats. Everyone's mood swings and changes. It's a constant case study in human behaviour, and all the chemical make-ups of those onboard,' observed boat trip veteran Tom wisely.

Sure enough, as the swell dropped, our crew went to town on the four- to six-foot rights regardless, with skis and tow boards, and very nearly created a whole new sport. It might not be the purist's cup of tea, but the possibilities opened up in small to medium surf with the skis and foot straps is mind-boggling. One afternoon, Dave and Kelly put on a show that resembled those video surfing games where you merrily spin the little man through quadruple aerial 360s for maximum points. With his windsurfing background, Dave has the aerial flip thing wired and, teamed up with Kelly and his aerial expertise, the pair went mad.

Whipping each other into peaks from the shoulder, they'd pull 50-metre cutbacks, 10-metre air drop floaters over six-foot barrels, and all manner of spinning aerial dismounts, swooping on each other with the ski and towing back out for more before you could blink. I saw surfing manoeuvres that have no names, that my brain could barely process. At one stage Kelly poured all his blistering speed into what I can only describe as an underwater cutback, deliberately burying himself and his board into the wave face in the mouth of the tube, somehow winding up laying back in the barrel with the nose of his board pointed at the lip, before coolly whipping the board back under him and riding out of the thing. 'You can get a little sloppy with straps because it's so easy to recover,' he noted afterwards, ever the perfectionist.

'I've never surfed with straps before in small waves so I'm just learning what's possible,' Kelly reflected later, obviously excited by the potential. 'How many sessions do you have when you say, "I wish I was over there, I wish I was over there?" Now you can be a hundred metres away in five seconds.'

'All the stuff that's possible in snowboarding is possible with straps,' Dave reckoned. He and his mates have been towing in small waves for years, pulling full loop aerials like windsurfers, and expecting the whole strapped-in small-wave thing to take off. But the young aerial kids remain either uninterested, or unaware, of the strapped-in potential.

'It's peer pressure, it's not fashionable. But it is the future,' Dave predicted. Dave uses straps even without a ski and can nimbly slip his feet into the straps every time.

If young Dylan is anything to go by, the next generation could adopt the strapped-in thing in a big way. 'Dave and Kelly doing tow-ins, doing those flip twist things, those things are crazy. I don't even know how they think of doing those things,' he gushed.

This was all good and fine, but it was not why we'd come here. You can hardly pretend to be boldly going where no surfer has gone before, when there's a mini-United Nations of fellow surfers camped on the beach. And while they'd enjoyed the show, after a couple of days the ski was going to wear a bit thin with them, even if it stuck to the outside bombs. Thus we set off into two days of rain and small swell. The DVD players got a thrashing. 'Snatch' was the hit pick of the week — the pommy 'Pulp Fiction'-ish gangster spoof — and soon Ross and Tom were jabbering away all day in thick cockney accents, calling everyone 'Turkish' out of the corner of their mouths. We pulled the classic surf check run-around — you know the one — where you drive around all day and end up back where you started. 'Is that where we've been surfing? I feel like we should be in Sri Lanka by now,' Ross observed, squinting over at the familiar, lumpy lineup after hours of motoring about neighbouring islands.

The rain let up, eventually, so Tom and Kelly went diving, while Ross, Dave and Pete bravely fronted up for the dreaded interview session, with no fewer than three cameras trained on them as they discussed their big wave deeds. Pete is a classic, a big friendly lumberjack of a fellow, conceived in Hawaii, where his dad shaped boards in Mokuleia while his mum sold Avon, and born in Santa Cruz after his parents moved there and opened a surf shop. 'The shop, my bedroom and the shaping bay were all right next to each other,' Pete reminisced fondly.

They did their jobs beautifully for the cameras and, as I looked at these three likeable blokes laughing and joking, it was tough to equate them with the images you see of the brave matadors taking off on the most monstrous waves ever ridden.

At what size does tow surfing get serious, the interviewer wanted to know.

'It's more fun from 20 to 25 feet, beyond that it gets pretty serious,' said Ross.

'There are days that are 30 feet and it's breaking perfectly,' Dave enthused. 'But I don't know if there's such a thing as a fun 30 feet.' He laughed, then grew serious for a moment. 'You've got to be focused and a little bit careful. And ride. Make it. Don't fall.'

What's next?

'They'll be finding others soon. People like myself are looking at all the maps and charts,' Pete reckoned.

'You can just follow these big red spots around the planet,' Ross exclaimed gleefully, talking about the colour-coded swell maps that indicate 60-foot seas with red blobs.

There was a wonderful moment, mid-interview, when a local 'feral' fishing boat chugged by with eight or so surfers on board, as our big-wave guys fronted the cameras on the rear deck of the mighty *Indies Trader*. There was no weird vibe, just understanding smiles between these fellow surfers at opposite ends of the surf trip spectrum.

One morning, I notice a strange warning sticker on one of the jet skis. 'Strong streams of water from the jet nozzle can be dangerous and can result in serious injury when directed at the body orifices (rectum and vagina).' Well, it had honestly never occurred to me, but I guess if you were stuck out here long enough . . .

We anchor in a beautiful bay, islands dotted everywhere, but precious little swell. I lose track of time, days even. One night I open my eyes from a deep sleep and through the porthole I see a gleaming blue vessel cruise up alongside and hear a great clamour of greetings. It's the *Indies Trader III*, the latest addition to Martin's fleet, a vessel of such opulence and luxury that a berth goes for around US$400 per person, per night. I stumble out of my cabin to see what the commotion is. Martin is standing right there in front of me on the deck of his new toy, grinning from ear to ear, extending a hand and, before I can wipe the sleep from my eyes, he's yanked me aboard and transported me to another world — a world where you might expect to find Hugh Hefner scuffing around in his pyjamas and slippers, and Playboy bunnies draped about the furniture. There's carpet throughout, a huge leather lounge, a grand dining table with seats for twelve, a timber-panelled bar with every spirit imaginable in stock, queen-sized beds with ensuites, and a huge map of the world occupying one whole wall of the main living area. It's currently occupied by a bunch of good ol' American boys, fiftyish surf dogs who must have somehow struck it rich. And Darrick, grinning away, along for the ride. The bourbon and cokes are flying about, Creedence is cranking on the stereo and I get the grand tour, feeling like I'm in a dream.

Darrick is wary about the tow-in thing when he hears the boys have been using the jet skis. 'Could you paddle in?' he quizzes me, earnestly. 'Were there other guys out?' The answer is yes to both. 'Be careful with that,' he warns seriously, brow furrowing with concern. 'You've seen the monster we've created at home. Six-foot Backyards, skis buzzing eveywhere.'

When I wake up in the morning the *Indies III* is gone and I wonder whether I dreamt the whole thing, except that Martin is now on our boat, and he wasn't yesterday.

The days melt into one another. Island after island, bay after bay, reefs after headlands. I have no idea where we are. Albert's secrets are safe. It's baking hot, not a breath of wind. Flying fish scatter and skim across the sheet-glass water in our wake. A few of the beaches we stop at are covered in turtle nests, the tracks of the prospective mothers criss-crossing the sand. The swell is still small. We come across a nice right-hand point, two to three feet, but peeling for hundreds of metres. There's another yacht here, and a couple of people surfing. Like the fish, empty waves are harder to come by than they once were.

It's good to get wet and the yachties seem fine with company — a guy and four girls on board. He's a merchant seaman who works for six months, then sails for six months. How does he happen to be here on a yacht, surfing perfect waves with four women, I have to ask.

'I could tell you I'm hung like a horse,' he laughs, before revealing the true story. His girlfriend and her buddies helped him paint and renovate his yacht up in Thailand, so he promised to take them to this secret spot as a reward, on the strict condition that they never breathed a word of it to anyone. They'd been here two hours when we rocked up.

'It takes a lot of effort, but when you're sitting out in the water somewhere like here it's worth every penny,' he tells me. The three single women, zapping about in their Zodiac or sunbaking on the beach in bikinis, naturally hold no interest to the vast majority of our crew — in happy committed relationships. The one single man aboard, Guy the cook on *Indies II*, however, bakes them muffins and paddles them over to their yacht on a bodyboard. 'That's not a good look,' Ross warns. 'At least take a surfboard.'

The right-hand point is fun, gentle, not real hollow, but very rippable. The surf comes up a couple of feet the next day and everyone has a ball. Kelly's surfing is outrageous. He's trying to perfect his aerial flips and lands a couple on the back of the wave — he's up there for so long the wave has passed by the time he gets back down. One late arvo session, as the sun sets and the sky does its thing, small purple and gold fish swim about us in the lineup, neatly mirroring the colours of the twilight. One appears to be trying to play with Kelly, nipping and pecking at him and then ducking away when he tries to catch it with cupped hands. It must be attracted to the colours of his board, I suggest. 'I think we've got something special going on, me and the fish,' Kelly reckons.

The *Indies I* lifts anchor and moves down the point to find a safe place to moor for the night, and all of a sudden our only lineup spot is gone. There is nothing but earth, sea and sky, and I suddenly feel quite tiny. The tinnie comes to collect us as the stars blink on like streetlights.

And so it goes on. Serious swell looks at least a week away, and a decision is made to extend the trip. One boat has to return to port, but the other is going to stay out and wait for waves, however long it takes, and the crew must split up. Tom, Dave, Ry and a few of us media people head back early, while the others bunker down on *Indies I* for the long haul.

We surf a super fun left on the way home that kind of makes the trip for me, and then say our goodbyes. The others will score a series of stunning lefts barrelling over shallow reef in the days ahead, as the swell finally kicks in and they get to do their thing — Kelly finally landing a flip, before spraining his ankle trying it in straps. I could be bummed but I'm not, just grateful for the time at sea.

Hell, these charter boats might be the soft option, and I salute the crew who do it tough under their own steam — the hardships they endure, the self-awareness they must cultivate. And the inevitable spread of surf tourism will continue to encroach upon some people's private slices of paradise. But somehow, if we can just learn to tread softly, I feel that the more people who get to sit out here for a couple of weeks of their life, even just once, and see and feel what it's like to bob around on a boat or camp out on a magical tropical island — seeing the flying fish and the jungle and the sunsets and the spinning reef waves — the better off we'll all be. I always feel subtly changed after time on a boat. I come home and see everything through fresh eyes, like some part of me dissolves and something new arises in its place, out there on the water.

I'm genuinely amazed how cool the other travellers we encountered were, showing no hint of territorialism and happy to enjoy the show — even with our media entourage and jet skis and live internet feeds. And I hope we did no harm. Out there it all seemed so simple, reduced to basic necessities and urges: find waves, anchor, surf, eat, sleep, do it again, or move on. If only life could be like that . . .

First published in *Surfing Life* magazine, 2001

3

PLACES IN THE MIND

Hitching a ride with Wayne Lynch when the swell's up on the Victorian coast can take you places you never imagined

Andrew Kidman

I'd been trying to photograph Wayne Lynch surfing for a month. I'd waited around for swells to come and winds to shift. For banks to form and professional surfers to move on.

That night I drove down to Wayne's house; he wasn't home when I arrived, but his wife Lindy assured me he'd be home sometime later. I was burned and crashed outside in one of the caravans that live on his block.

I woke early in the morning and walked down the driveway to check the swell. Wayne's car was in so I knew he was home.

The sun drenched the morning in one massive orange curtain while a ten-foot swell killed the beaches. It was hard to tell where the world went round, where the water touched the air, what were waves and what were clouds. Only the bush scrub I stood in gave it any perspective at all.

I walked back up to the house and went in. 'There you are,' Wayne said, somewhat surprised. 'I've been looking for you everywhere, ringing everywhere, waking up everyone in Torquay.'

I told him I'd been asleep in the caravan. He knew the swell was up and the winds were right, but we had to wait for his friend and tow partner Glen Casey to get a family outing organised before we could all head down the coast. Wayne paced the house for the next hour muttering about it being one of those days, then he rang Case again. Case was organising the tea and cookies and was nearly ready. More stomping of the floorboards and so on. I sat there saying nothing. I'd seen it all before. I wasn't surprised in the slightest.

By 9.30 we had the boat hooked up and were on the road. It's a two-hour drive down the coast, maybe longer. I've done it so many times I can't remember anymore, if that makes any sense. We met Case on the road at the petrol station. He had the jet ski, his girlfriend, his girlfriend's sister and her boyfriend in tow. He grinned like he always does. Case's grin covers every other thought he's having. I'm sure he was having a few other thoughts that morning that had nothing to do with the look on his face.

By the time we reached the coast, we'd managed to lose Case. Wayne and I pulled into the lookout over the big bay to check the swell. It was 15 feet, probably bigger. It was a strong swell, wrapping into the bay, the biggest I'd ever seen down there. There was a weird rip in the channel that was forcing it to close out. It had started to rain and it was cold. I tried not to think about what Wayne could want me to do this day. There were two surfers in the lineup. One of them was Tony Ray. He rode a wave from the takeoff. He dodged the falls of water that tossed themselves at him, he turned and hung in under the lip line, then he turned again and moved into the channel, a successful ride. It was a brilliant piece of big wave surfing.

Wayne was hopping mad by this time. The swell was chunky and Case was nowhere to be seen. We drove up to the top car park to find him. It was lined with surfers' cars checking the swells. So much for a low-key area. A massive set poured through. Tony Ray and the other rider began their defensive plans to outwit the beast. It sucked on another outer reef as the riders pressed their chests to the decks and were lifted in the swell. It sucked hard and went black on its own shadow; they remained stagnant in its pinnacle. Teetering, they fell on the backside while the wave hollowed itself and exploded on the reef. I could only think about being sucked over and drowning, or being caught inside, as Tony Ray's brother Michael walked down the cliff with his gun under his arm.

Case was nowhere to be seen. Someone might have noticed him at some other check spot so we drove to it. He was out there grinning. So was the rest of the big wave crowd. We walked out onto the bluff that overlooked about six outer reefs. All fanning off in the wind, the swells taking their time to find the reefs and rise up. They were big, dark, perfect waves. There was a lot of pointing going on.

Lynch's, a giant left that Wayne pioneered with Maurice Cole, was doing its thing. The swell looked too big for it, but sometimes it would reel off. A perfect wave. It was hard to tell really where the reef was, where it would consistently line up and break. It didn't seem to have any set pattern and the sets looked like they were closing out. But then there would be another perfect one. There seemed like two swells, but who could tell? The magnitude of it all was confusing enough.

Someone asked Wayne if he was going out. 'I'm going out and I'm going to tow in,' he said sternly under his hood in the rain. Case and I just looked at each other, grinless. It was serious now and the day was moving on. It was only a matter of time before we'd be dealing with the waves we were watching. We made tracks for the boat ramp.

Wayne was on auto now. He powered to the ramp, which was just a slippery, dogged descent of about a hundred metres to the ocean. He backed the car up and dropped the boat over the edge. It bounced its way down on the trailer to the sandy beach at the bottom. Three-foot waves swelled in the little bay and rushed the shore. The worn cliffs hung around in the descending grey; they'd seen days like this before. While out, off in the ocean, the sandstone pillars disturbed the run of the swells, cutting up slabs of draining water and torrents of swirling white chaos. It was not a place any sane man was going.

We loaded the boat up and dropped the jet ski in. Case was on the ski and Wayne was driving the duckie. The girlfriends waved goodbye as the boyfriend watched on.

Oh well, whatever, I thought. I'd been in situations like this before and figured it was just a matter of dealing with it, riding it out. The one thing I'd learned about boats was: if it can go wrong it will and to be prepared for anything. I hung on to the front rope with a death-white grip as we battered our way out through the crazy sandstone pillars.

Barely past one of the larger ones, the motor on the boat conked out. The boat stopped, lifting from all directions as it bounded in the wash; behind us this huge wraith of vertical earth drawing us back toward it. Wayne was down on the motor, the fuel line had popped off and it was only a matter of clipping it back on and pumping the fuel in. There's usually some kind of delay as the fuel works its way through the line. Wayne ripped the cord and it started first go. We zoomed from the shadow of the beast, dodging swells and cross chop, out into the glass of the offshore deep.

Like a bird. Like an albatross riding the waves — that's how Wayne always described surfing in his boat. He was following the swells now, and running them down. Then he'd run back up them and out off the side, drawing on the swell line, then driving back off it, drifting and planing along the face, kissing some kind of weightlessness. My head had only a sense of itself, feeling the wind without a body, taking on the eyes of a bird. Feeling the swells. Sitting to the side of the boat felt like this. The swells were giant, fat and long. Sometimes they'd steepen up as they approached the reefs, and Wayne would angle down them, seeing how far he could push it before it all got too tight. Then he'd glide back out and hunt another, more alive than I'd ever seen him, excited, somewhere else.

We approached Lynch's. Case was already up there checking it out with the jet ski. It was a lot like it looked from the land, shifting up and down the reef with the different swells, though the whole deal had a totally new perspective now. We were in the ballpark, watching swells break past us and rising on swells that would break if they were any bigger. And who was to say they wouldn't get any bigger or come in from a different direction? I was starting to feel quite nervous about the whole situation. We were a long way out to sea. There was a 15-foot swell running and it could at any time decide it was bigger — it was not coherent. It was raining and we were sitting off the reef where Wayne once saw Big Ben, the biggest great white shark he's ever seen. And he didn't mind telling the story either.

Just trying to locate the left was a problem. At one stage we thought we were on it, checking it for viability. Wayne was watching the other way and I was looking out to sea when this mass peak reared up and began chasing us down. I yelled to Wayne. He turned in time to hit the throttle and power off to the right shoulder of the wave. There was no time to do anything else as we launched off the side of it and down its back, only to be confronted by the second wave of the set and to do it all again.

I'm not sure where Wayne was taking his bearings from, but after a while he reckoned he had a spot to anchor the boat on the reef where the waves wouldn't break. Truthfully, I was not so sure. Case and Wayne geared up for the tow. Case was on the ski and Wayne was surfing. They powered out to the left and I sat in the boat. I was alone now and talking to myself, sometimes to God. The whole thing had bent my mind into some other realm, a crazy realm of giggling and screaming, then to another realm of quiet, still ease.

I watched as Case towed Wayne into a swell. It looked like he was standing on the top of a mountain, but the swell wasn't big enough to break and it passed by him. Directly behind it was a giant set and Wayne was smack bang in the impact zone. The set drilled him, as did the ten waves that followed. Case was looking for him among the foam, while I was watching the white water dissipate just in time to miss the boat. I knew then it was only a matter of time before I got cleaned up.

Case found Wayne and brought him back out. I told them the waves were coming pretty close to the boat, but they were excited now by the tow and said it would be all right. Then they zoomed off.

This was one of the eeriest moments in my life. I sat on the side of the boat, on a dead calm, grey ocean. The quiet was sickening. Then a swell would come and the boat would rise up on it. And with it a chattering from the wind, as the droplets from the top of the wave got caught in the wind and were lifted back, landing on the water. The bigger the swell the louder the chattering, then nothing. Just still again. All the time waiting. All the time knowing that it wouldn't be long. I was ready for it too. I had my wetsuit on and my camera in its housing and I knew I was just going to jump overboard and get away from the boat as soon as that wave came in.

Once again Case towed Wayne into the first wave of the set and the wave again outran Wayne and he was cleaned up by the rest of the set. This time the set was bigger than the previous one and it made its way toward me. I sat on the side of the boat watching the wave about to mow it down. Moments before it hit, I leapt overboard as the wave totalled the duckie.

When I surfaced, it was upside down. The gear was everywhere, bags and clothes, tool kits, a helmet. Case's tow board. It was all strewn through the lineup. Wayne and Case were still inside being beaten by the set. I sat in the water trying to figure out what to do. The brain had flopped over into some other realm now. It was thinking survival. No panic, just even thoughts. 'Get the gear to the boat, try to get it all.' I swam around collecting what I could, keeping my eye on the ocean outside. I had the board up on the upturned hull and the tool kit, when I looked outside to the biggest wave I'd seen capping and coming directly at the boat. It was all now in the impact zone. My main fear was getting entangled in the anchor rope, so I swam under the boat and to the ocean side of it. The wave broke. I took a photo of it and dived under. The beast belted me, turning me on my head and spinning me upside down. When I surfaced, I had no idea where I was, totally disoriented. I looked around to see the boat some fifty metres away from me. I soon realised I was way out the back. The gear was nowhere and everywhere. Case and Wayne were onto me in a second.

The survival thing kicked in again: 'Get the boat out of the impact zone.' I passed Case the camera and he put it in the ski. Wayne and I pulled the boat over and he began working the anchor free from the reef, sending Case and me to find the gear. We spent the next half hour outrunning ten-foot peeling walls looking for the thousand dollar virgin tow board. In the process, we found a helmet and a bag. In a burst of panic we thought about Wayne, and went out to see where he was at with the boat. He was way outside the lineup. He had the oars out and he was rowing. It is still one of the funniest things I've ever seen. We left him to it.

We went back inside, hugging the cliffs, searching for the bright red board among the chaos. Then Case saw it, caught in a rip by one of the cliffs. We darted over and picked it up. The beach was close by and never looked so good. I thought we should try and put the gear up in the bushes and go out and help Wayne, so we did. When I was walking back down the beach, trying to get my head around going out in the ocean again, Wayne came zooming through the break. Somehow he'd got the motor started. We were going home — what a relief! I got the gear, got back in the boat and we headed off to the boat ramp.

It was a rough ride home, but it didn't seem to matter. Wayne was spewing. He was spewing about the waves he was missing and the jacket he'd lost. We made it back to the sandy beach and

Case came back in on the jet ski. Then Wayne put it on us. 'We're going back out. There's enough light left, we're going back out.' I couldn't believe it, but knew he was serious. The girlfriends and boyfriend couldn't believe it either. They'd just watched it all from the cliff, and now we were refuelling and going back out to do it all again. It was cold and dark as we headed back out. I had the shivers up, but I seemed to be getting used to the idea. The idea of being deliriously mad, of having no control. The idea that nothing mattered anyway.

Wayne anchored the boat way out to sea this time. The chills were back as the boat rose in the swells, but it would take the mother of them all to flip it this far out. Wayne was on the ski now, towing Case. They dropped me off near the lineup so I could photograph it. I was sitting on Wayne's fluoro yellow tow board, submerged up to my stomach from the weight, a lure, a prime target for any fish that might need a feed. I felt at this time that I knew exactly what Big Ben looked like. I could see his eyes as they came from the deep, hammering me into space. The mind went into the realm of hysteria and out beyond. I just sat there shivering, watching Wayne tow Case into these giant waves. It was surrealism in its highest form.

The dark was setting in now, it was still raining, and there was little definition between anything out on the sea. Some black birds flew home in the calm, while raindrops painted flawless oscillations on the smooth grey blanket. Outside, the biggest wave I'd seen all day honked onto the reef and Wayne was towing Case into it. He charged from behind the peak and across, then down the line as the wave folded over. Case looked like an ant as it wrapped around and engulfed him. Wayne was on the wave behind it on the jet ski, an even bigger wave; he looked like a cowboy charging down the face, screaming his head off. The wave cleaned me up and I lost his board.

He collected it for me and I hinted that maybe we could go in now, that I felt a little like shark bait sitting out here on my own. He said 'Just a couple more', and was gone. But another wave never really came before it got too dark. They came over to pick me up and I started laughing at them, saying, 'Ahh, don't worry about it, I'll just hang out here all night.' So Wayne left me there and took Case out to the boat. I sat there in the dark — mindless. Case came back to get me and I jumped off the jet ski when we got near the boat. I was drifting in the water when Wayne barked an order at me: 'Hey, don't mess around out there, mate. I'm serious. I told you this is where I saw that shark.' I got in the boat.

We surfed like birds on the swells on the way home. We ducked in behind the giant black ogres and headed for the little sandy beach. It was pissing down now, the girls were sitting in the car and the boyfriend was out on the winch putting all his muscle into getting the boat up. He was a legend. He had the strength of ten of me. We had the strength of none.

I remember standing on the beach in the dark watching the silver rain fall past the brake lights of Wayne's 4WD as he hooked it up over the ramp and disappeared up the hill. He was a maniac, but he'd pulled it off. We were all safe.

We dried off our bodies out in front of the local general store/bottle-oh. It was the first time we'd been dry in about eight hours. It felt good. We got some hot chips and beer, waved goodbye to Case and his load, and started driving the two hours home in the dark. The heater felt good, although later down the road Wayne told me it wasn't working.

First published in the *Surfers Journal*, 1998.

4

GODS OF THE SEA

Were the Polynesians really the first surfers, or could ancient Peruvian fishermen have a claim to the title?

Matt Griggs

For Australians, surfing started in 1914, when the legendary Hawaiian surfer, Duke Kahanamoku (gold medal swimmer and three-time world record holder in the 100-metre freestyle), gave surf-riding demonstrations on a summer day at Freshwater Beach in Sydney.

For Duke, it started in 1905 as a teenager in Hawaii.

For Hawaii, the traditional custodian of surfing culture and history, it was discovered by Captain Jimmy Cook, and recorded in his journal, in 1779. But petroglyphs of surfers, carved into lava rocks in Hawaii, date surfing back as early as AD 1500. The line of surfing history stops there, like a wave to shore. But a new source of evidence reveals a wave-riding culture whose mystery runs as deep as the ocean itself. So when did surfing start? The answer may lie buried in the sandy coastal desert of Peru, in South America.

Here, pre-Inca ceramics dating back to 600 BC show the earliest evidence so far of wave riding. This newfound evidence takes the origins of wave riding back at least 2600 years. That's around 1000 years before Hawaii was even settled.

'Why not?' says Roberto Meza Vallue, as he holds a small replica of what could possibly be the world's first surfboard. He pauses and examines the surfboard-like curves as if it were his own new board.

At normal size, the woven reed vessels are between nine and 15 feet (roughly three to five metres) in length and around two feet (60 centimetres) wide. They have two cylindrical sections like a catamaran with no gap, whose nose thins out and curves upwards into a wild-rocker (the banana shape of a modern surfboard — only realised in surfboard shaping in the past two decades). They are called *cabaui to de totoras*, in Spanish, which translates to 'horse of reeds'.

'But it is pre-Inca, pre-Christian . . . pre-everything,' explains Roberto with a twinkle of pride. His olive skin and wild surfer's hair suggests a mix of Indian and Spanish blood. A former surfing champion and big-wave specialist, Roberto is helping in the research for a book on the history of surfing in Peru. 'Modern surfing may have started in Hawaii,' he says. 'But when did wave riding start?'

It's a question that has me diving deep into a mysterious culture — and through the back streets of a city more dangerous than any lineup, Lima.

'These totora sea horses [reed vessels] were used for fishing,' says Javier Fernandez, editor of *Tablista*, Peru's surfing magazine. He also keeps a small model of a totora in his downtown Lima office. 'There are not many channels [breaks in the waves] in Peru,' he explains. 'So the people would kneel down and paddle them through the surf to fish in deeper waters. When they came in at the end of the day they would stand up on the totoras and ride the wave in standing up.'

Ceramics dating back 1200 years show smaller versions of the totoras which were paddled like today's surfboards. These scaled-down versions, perhaps seven feet in length, were designed for days when the surf was big and the larger totoras were hard to get out the back. The craftsmanship of these artefacts shows incredible wave knowledge and surfboard design insights.

'For sure, they were right into surfing,' says Magoo de la Rosa Toro, seven-time Peruvian surfing champion, who has enough gold in his trophy cabinet to rival the Inca royal family. At thirty-six, Magoo's energy and passion for surfing are unrivalled. So too is his passion for history. His backyard houses the seeds of a future surfboard museum, including totoras. 'Look at them,' he says, 'they have perfect rocker — they were way better designed for surfing than for fishing.'

A board paddler can be seen in the foreground of this scene depicting the arrival of Captain James Cook at Kealakekua, Hawaii, in 1779. This picture is a part of a larger engraving by the artist to the expedition, John Webber.

The first known western drawing of surfing, by F. Howard, from *Polynesian Researches During a Residence of Nearly Eight Years in the Society and Sandwich Islands*, published in 1831.

TONY MORRISON/SOUTH AMERICAN PICTURES

An ancient image of a Peruvian fisherman apparently surfing, on a balsa (known today as a *caballito totora* or reed boat) from the Mochica culture, on Peru's desert coast, circa 400 AD.

TONY MORRISON/SOUTH AMERICAN PICTURES

A Peruvian fisherman paddles through the surf on his reed boat, or *caballito totora*, at Huanchacho. Was this the beginning of surfing?

Newspix/News Ltd
Newspix/News Ltd

LEFT: Duke Kahanamoku, Hawaiian swimming and surfing champion, surrounded by beachgoers after his historic surfing demonstration at Manly in 1915. RIGHT: Nearly fifty years later, fourteen-year-old Leslie McDiamond at Coogee shows how Australians have taken to the surf.

LEROY GRANNIS

Miki Dora shows the cool style that made him the benchmark at Malibu in the '50s and '60s.

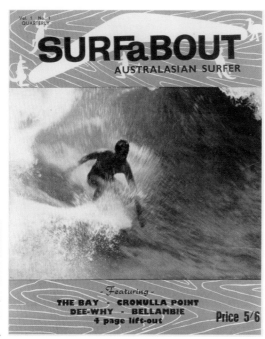

JACK EDEN/SURFABOUT COLLECTION

The first cover of *Surfabout*, Australia's second surfing magazine, depicting a daring nose ride at Bellambi Pier, near Corrimal, NSW. The magazine sold out all 10 000 copies in three days.

JACK EDEN/SURFABOUT COLLECTION

Looking like James Dean by the beach, well-known surfer and board builder Gary Birdsall is a study of surfer nonchalance, at Bellambi in 1959.

JACK EDEN/SURFABOUT COLLECTION

JACK EDEN/SURFABOUT COLLECTION

ABOVE: Bobby Brown carves a smooth bottom turn at Sandon Point in 1965, as surfing's popularity swept the coast. LEFT: Kevin Parkinson toes on nose in '66 — the style that held local grommets in awe.

JACK EDEN/SURFABOUT COLLECTION

A packed Bellambi car park for the NSW South Coast Championships in 1965, as surfing's growth gave rise to competition and clubs.

Kelly Slater flies above the wave during a surfing expedition to remotest Indonesia.

Ry Craike floats over shallow reef, somewhere off the coast of Sumatra, Indonesia, and a long way from the nearest medical help.

GLEN DUFFUS

A nice bunch of boys to take home to meet mum — the 'Bra Boys. 'Ride with us or collide with us', is their motto.

DAVE SPARKES

Head 'Bra Boy Koby Abberton doing what he does best, and where he's least likely to find trouble.

ANDREW KIDMAN

ANDREW KIDMAN

Two evocative results of wind on water — airbrushed swell lines buffet the Victorian coastline.

Later that week we were watching two locals paddle out on their totoras at Huanchaco (north of Lima). The surfers turned around and caught the wave while still on their knees, then stood up and manoeuvred with their oars towards the shore, finally riding waves in. 'They are hard to ride,' admitted Magoo. 'You have to turn them with the oar — that's like their fin.'

The biggest thing I noticed was the smile on each rider's face. 'There's no way they just used them for fishing,' said Magoo. 'Look at him. Look how happy he is. Who can catch just one wave and then come in?'

Archeologists and historians believe that the totora sea horses were used by high chiefs, as well as common people, for competitions in both wave-riding and paddling events. But so little is known and so much is yet to be discovered that the locals are not the only ones theorising.

'This is just the earliest evidence to date,' says Magoo. 'I think the cabaui to de totoras are at least 5000 years old. They have just found remains of fishing nets that date to that time.' He paused, allowing the obvious answer to stir. 'Where do you catch bigger fish, or where do you use fishing nets? Further out. How do you get there? With a boat. What is the only boat used by the pre-Incas? The cabaui to de totoras. How do you get in? You catch waves.'

I go to see another expert. 'I was in Huanchaco five years ago,' says Adolfo Valderrama Bielich, who perhaps offers the most informed voice on the subject. He is a 46-year-old economist, teacher and surfer. 'It was a good day for surfing,' he continues. 'I spoke to an old indigenous fisherman. We were watching the surfers and he was saying, "I remember doing that when I was a child." He told me how his father used to speak of riding the waves when he was a child also.'

But as with the grommets of today, the pre-Inca grommets' first 'boards' were hand-me-downs. 'The totoras only have a life span of sixty days,' says Adolfo. He points to his own surfboard, yellow with age and I imagine the totora reeds softening and losing their drive. 'After that period they would pass them down to the kids to develop their ocean skills. There were also special totoras made for competitions where the elders could show *their* skills.'

When the Spanish Conquistadors arrived in northern Peru in 1528, they observed something they had never before witnessed — surfing. One Spanish wordsmith made this poetic entry in his ship's log:

> . . . native gliding over the ocean on what seemed to be graceful sea horses. They cut through the water, advancing with their long necks propelled forward with an easy rhythm of grace and beauty. Indeed a beautiful sight to behold, as they dance over the swells. They return with the waves and the foam, as carefree as musical notes in a pagan celebration. At times they seem totally lost among the breakers, only to reappear as if engaged in a game with the sea. As sunset roars, they return toward shore for their last ride. A lovely sight in the fresh and golden sunlight.

However, the Spanish amigos were not the only seafaring people sailing the unmapped seas of the world — and here comes the link to Hawaii. Genetic, trade and mythological connections between the Polynesian and Peruvian peoples date back even further. It seems likely that the Peruvians passed on their knowledge of wave riding to the Polynesians and by extension the Hawaiians — in fact the Polynesians may have been direct descendants of the ancient Peruvians.

'It goes even deeper,' says Adolfo. 'They have found traces of cocaine and tobacco on Egyptian mummies dating back 4000 years. These products only came from Peru. Sweet potato is found in Hawaii now, called "kumara". This is a Quechua word from Peru dating back more than 5000 years. There is no doubt that these Pacific people had connection with each other, but the question is, who made first contact between the world's first surfers, and when?'

Hidden in the desert around the world-famous area of Chicama (the world's longest left-hander), is evidence of wave riding and ocean exploration by pre-Inca civilisations. The pre-Inca ruins at first glance may appear to be one of the many rocky sand dunes that characterise the desert coast, such is their magnificent height and rugged harmony with the surrounding landscape. But these are not natural. They are the 'Temples of the Sun and Moon' — two pre-Inca pyramids only recently discovered. On their muralled walls are not only endless pictures of waves, but stylised images of surfing as well.

On one such wall in the ruins of El Brujo in Trujillo, near Chicama, is an illustration depicting crude latitude and longitude representations, and various fish that travel in uniform patterns. This feature is believed by some to be a map of the South Pacific.

'They say the Polynesians came to Peru first,' says Adolfo. 'But it was the other way around. We have the proof.'

On 28 April 1947, the Norwegian explorer Thor Heyerdahl (who died fairly recently) set out from the seaport of Callao in Peru on a craft named *Kon Tiki* ('The Sun God'), in an attempt to retrace the mythical voyages of the ancient Peruvians. He also set out to show that the Polynesians could in fact be descendants of the pre-Inca Peruvians. Using no navigational equipment, he rode the currents to Polynesia, arriving in 101 days. This demonstrated that the Inca rafts, and rafts of previous civilisations, could well have reached places as far away as the Galapagos, Easter Island, French Polynesia and New Zealand.

It also supports the theory that by the time the Polynesians sailed for Hawaii the islands had already been reached by the Peruvians. But aboard these rafts were people who took with them more than trade and ideas of expansion — they took wave riding.

'I propose this,' says Adolfo in his simplest breakdown. 'The ancient Peruvians were surfing without doubt in AD 300. That's 700 years before Hawaii was even settled. If you believe the fishing nets are proof of surfing also, then they were surfing at least 5400 years before Hawaii was even settled.'

Surfing has transfixed people ever since, not least Captain Cook. 'The boldness and address, with which we saw them perform these difficult and dangerous manoeuvres, was altogether astonishing, and is scarcely to be credited,' he said of his experience in Hawaii.

The Hawaiians took their 'Sport of Kings' to the world like a fresh new groundswell. In 1885 three Hawaiian princes visiting Santa Cruz in California, were reported to have ridden waves at the San Lorenzo river mouth on boards shaped from local redwood.

Duke Kahanamoku passed through southern California en route to the summer Olympics in Stockholm, Sweden. His surfing demonstrations at Corona del Mar and Santa Monica caused a sensation. Touted as the fastest swimmer alive, Duke was on the road constantly, giving swimming exhibitions around Europe, the United States and the rest of the world.

So when did surfing start? The history books will tell you Hawaii. When did wave riding start? The Peruvians will argue Peru. One thing's for certain, buried beneath the sands of Peru's coastal desert lies concrete evidence of wave riding, originating from a culture that treasured the ocean long before modern surfing took off in Hawaii.

With its long pointbreaks and magnificent landscapes, Peru has a special allure but there is also something mysterious and timeless about it. There are few trees there, but their roots seem to go on forever.

First published in *Tracks* magazine, 2002.

5

TACKLING GORILLAS IN PERU

In a dusty, desert town in Peru, surf travellers are driven to strange behaviour when deprived of waves

Tim Baker

'What's the circus like?' I asked our Peruvian hosts, desperate for some entertainment in this dusty, off-season holiday town.

'No, you don't want to go to the circus,' Fernando assured us seriously. Others joined in, suddenly impassioned.

'They say there is a lion,' the vivacious young Vanessa announced accusingly, 'but it is just a dog with a mane round its neck.'

'They say there is a gorilla,' joined in Javier, as if battling a common foe, 'but it is just a man in a suit.' He spat the last words out with some contempt.

'It is a very bad circus,' our hosts nodded in earnest waves of agreement.

We gringos — bored out of our minds and already reverting to flatulence as a source of amusement — just stared at each other in a blinding moment of spontaneous, synchronised thought: we have to go to the circus.

Emboldened by several cold, tall bottles of Crystal beer, we easily overpowered the excited protests of our hosts. A few hotel staff are no match for a group of bored surfers starved of waves and fed a few ales. We'd travelled here fuelled on stories of the world's longest left-hander, empty desert points, miles of unexplored coastline in a land steeped in surfing history. The reality we'd encountered was something else altogether.

We had sat like this, in the stark, concrete cantina of the Posada del Mirador, for only a few languid evenings, looking out over the sleepy rows of squat box-like houses that ringed the bay of San Bartolo. Yet, already, quaint amusement had turned to weary resignation. The Pacific Ocean had lain there stubbornly — grey, flat, shrouded in fog and stinking of fish — since our arrival. And life on land bared its awful truths all too plainly. Nothing happened in San Bartolo. And everyone was mad.

The local community insisted on informing on one another at every opportunity, until the entire population had been branded with accusations of mental instability.

'See that guy over there,' Javier would tell us in a conspiratorial huddle, indicating some nondescript passer-by. 'He is crazy. You can see it in his eyes.'

'That Javier,' Fernando, the genuinely insane manager of the Mirador, would hiss as he bent low over our breakfast table. 'He is a bit crazy. You can't believe too much of what he says.'

'That Fernando,' Javier would snort disbelievingly of his employer. 'He's crazy. You look in his eyes.'

Perhaps it was the weather. It never rained in San Bartolo, or along any of the desert coast of Peru. Some houses had no roofs, others only threadbare bamboo shading. It was over fifty years since any rain was last recorded, and dunes of grey-brown dirt drifted off into the distance as far as the eye could see.

Or perhaps it was the schizophrenic nature of the town itself which infected its populace. On summer holidays and weekends, San Bartolo was transformed into a bustling seaside playground for wealthy city dwellers from the capital, Lima, a hundred kilometres to the north. They occupied their smart, Mediterranean-style holiday houses proudly and overflowed noisily from bars and restaurants.

During the week and in winter, San Bartolo lay like a discarded toy, gathering dust and fraying at the seams. Shutters went down on drink and ice-cream stalls, bars and restaurants disappeared behind awnings. The town simply shut its eyes and went to sleep. Those that stirred went about only the dull, monotonous duties of daily San Bartolo life.

But a circus? This was not for the wealthy holiday crowds. This was the simple, time-honoured tradition of the townsfolk. Yet this somehow seemed to make it unfit for the eyes of visitors. The circus was the mad uncle stuffed in the attic ... and we wanted to meet him.

We set out into the night down the lanes of grey dust lined with white-painted rocks that served as roads in San Bartolo. Through a gridlike maze we scuffed, past families scattered about doorways and windows, the occasional television set occupying the air with its dull drone and silver-blue light.

Seeing we could not be stopped, Vanessa and Javier eagerly assumed an air of amused ridicule, sharing heartily with us the joke of the circus now. 'Yes, yes, the circus will be so funny,' Vanessa decided aloud.

As we drew closer to the sagging, patchwork big top, a trail of pedestrian traffic trickled towards it, a tinny, crackling loudspeaker urged the crowd on, and painted banners advertised the show's highlights. Lions and gorillas did indeed feature prominently in this promotional material but, in the paintings at least, they looked entirely genuine.

Several streams of humanity combined at the mouth of the tent and formed a small rabble, purchasing tickets and popcorn as they moved at a slow shuffle through the flap. The interior resembled a rough but intimate, moodily lit theatre. Half a dozen rows of tiered seating lined the perimeter, with scores of small kiddies' chairs arranged closest to the low stage.

The crackling loudspeaker kept up a brisk running commentary throughout the show, but onstage the performers bellowed thunderously without any electronic amplification. Several unremarkable acts trundled across the stage without great fanfare, but the audience roared approvingly at everything.

A hush fell, however, as a uniformed trainer struggled on stage, leading a clearly agitated gorilla by a chain and collar. Kiddies pressed back in their chairs. Even adults gasped in horror as the gorilla bounded about the stage, grabbing at its collar. Could they not see the conspicuous seams that ran down the length of the gorilla's arms and legs? Or were the parents simply joining in the pantomime for the sake of the children? In San Bartolo, it was impossible to tell.

The trainer looked helplessly out at the audience with an expression of pure terror as he led the gorilla about. When the gorilla finally wrestled its collar off, the trainer threw up his hands and fled. Kids were out of the seats now, their parents oohing and aahing in a low rumble.

The gorilla jumped from the stage and began a theatrical hopping run down the aisle that separated the tiered seating from the kiddies' chairs. Children were running for their lives, squealing and waving their arms.

I don't know if it was the sight of the panic-stricken children. Or the days of boredom. Or the several beers I'd slurped in the glow of the desert sunset. But . . . I was sitting in the front row of the tiered seating, with a fake gorilla running towards me, children scattering in terror, and there was only one irresistible, instinctive reflex in me. I leapt from my chair, cut a path through the tide of children stampeding towards me, dipped one shoulder, accelerated into a determined trot, and tackled the crazed circus beast about the waist. Years of Australian Rules football training in the art of the shirtfront had paid off. The impact of the shoulder knocked the wind out of him, and he wheezed helplessly as my arms locked around his middle.

He was surprisingly light and I easily hoisted the struggling primate over my shoulder. My companions reported from the rear view that my quarry waved its arms and legs in the air for a few violent spasms, before collapsing limply about my shoulder. Kiddies stopped in their tracks, turned and began to cheer. Their parents joined in. I marched down the aisle to the stage and returned the demoralised gorilla to its trainer. The pair shuffled off, their act ruined. As I swaggered back to my seat, small children formed a kind of impromptu guard of honour, gazing up in wonderment at this pale, foreign saviour. 'Superman, Superman,' several of them chorused gleefully. Scattered applause hummed through the crowd as I resumed my seat, to hearty backslaps from my fellow travellers.

Throughout the remainder of the show, the spotlight would be shone on us sporadically and clearly disparaging remarks would be made over the loudspeaker or by the clowns on stage, to uproarious laughter from the audience. Only one word was recognisable out of the excited Spanish babble. 'Gringos!' We squirmed uncomfortably, smiling nervously at our neighbours while they held their stomachs and guffawed at our expense, as if they might die.

It still puzzles me. I'm the sort of person who will never make a fuss at a restaurant — I'd gulp down deep fried ducks' beaks rather than suggest someone got my order wrong. For one magical evening in the depressed seaside backwater of San Bartolo, I was a hero. I have probably already passed into local folklore. We went on to find some of those desert points, explore some of that lonely coast, living in bamboo shacks we built on the beach. But that night in San Bartolo remains a personal highlight.

And herein lies the very essence of travel. To shed the constricting armour of your station in life at home. To become a 'gringo' or some other alien character in the eyes of a curious local people, and to feel the liberty of acting upon impulse, freed from the constricting expectations of others.

Then again, there are probably places where, if you tackle a fake circus gorilla you could wind up with a knife in your guts. Travel is simply a matter of tackling the right gorillas.

First published in *Deep* magazine, 1996.

6

CAPE FEAR!

A fatal shark attack sends a wave of fear through the South Australian surf community

DC Green

Greg the publican smiled grimly. 'If the locals want to talk, they'll find you soon enough.'

'Thanks.' I'd just been reminded how much I didn't want this assignment — partly because of my shark phobia, partly because of the vampiric nature of tracking down the grieving, but mostly because of the location of the first attack. The locals at Cactus Beach on the Great Australian Bight in South Australia are renowned as the most paranoid and protective in the land. They have scared off marauding surf-media trips to the point where most surf journalists I know won't even visit relatives in Adelaide. And here I was now, out the back of the nearby Penong Hotel in a room that couldn't be easier for a lynch mob to locate — just get pissed and turn left at the beer garden. Still, I was hoping and half assuming the locals would be pleased at all the tourist-deterring publicity; but as happens with assumptions, I wasn't even warm.

I checked the surf right where Cameron Bayes was taken. Despite the brisk onshore, there were waves. Bleak, empty waves. I staggered through the saltbush to the camp-ground. It was deserted but for a few scattered feral tents and two German women on a horror pilgrimage in a sparkling campervan with annex. I fronted three guys from Lorne drinking beers. Because of my rented Commodore, they thought I was an undercover cop.

'Yeah, we've been surfing this morning,' said one. 'Sharks don't worry us. They can't learn tricks or remember things like dogs. They're just dumb fish!'

'I'm lucky because I haven't got much imagination,' said his mate.

The Lorne guys didn't want to have their photos taken (no one in Cactus did).

'The locals have left us alone,' explained one, 'other than warning us not to take any photos of the surf, and the odd weird stare. So we wouldn't want to rile them.'

Back at the pub I had a few beers and a counter meal, fearing confrontation at any moment. Yet I met only non-surfing locals and the odd visitor passing through. The only bloke with all his front teeth intact was staying overnight, en route on a solo ultralight flight from Geraldton to his home town, Kingston. He was seventy.

'I used to surf,' admitted the publican, Greg Warrington. In 1975 one of Greg's grommet mates, Wade Shippard, swam out to meet a fishing boat at Port Sinclair. A great white bit off the boy's leg and he bled to death on the way to Ceduna Hospital. Greg, and a few other locals, haven't surfed since.

'Kill every fucking shark!' snorted a truckie who was listening at the bar.

At dawn, the Commodore skimmed back across the salt plains to Cactus. The surf was still empty and the sweep of beach devoid of all humanity. What was I doing? Later, in Penong, I fronted a local surfer businessman who agreed to speak to me — provided I didn't use his name or take his photo.

'I'm one of the accepted spokesmen for the hierarchy,' he explained. 'Zed' was rational with his theories, but still clearly spooked. Like most locals, he planned on staying out of the surf for a month. 'It's still bloody well out there, big as a station wagon!'

I read every report of the attack (the whole town had clippings). The gruesome details slowly coagulated, and often contradicted. At the general store I lucked into meeting a veteran local ('just call me Harry') who'd seen the whole attack.

'The shark was so close to the beach, it looked artificial,' Harry reckoned.

'How big?' I asked.

The man's voice shook. 'Big as a caravan.'

New Zealanders Cameron and Tina Bayes were seven months into a working honeymoon holiday. Cameron had planned to surf a bit at Cactus before heading across the Nullarbor to find seasonal shearing work in Western Australia. On Sunday morning, 24 September 2000 the 25-year-old rose early to avoid the crowd. He'd already racked up about half a dozen good lefts by the time other surfers began to pull out their wetsuits, including a carload of school children.

At 7.30am a great white launched itself completely out of the water at the Cactus end section — seemingly the shallowest, least likely place in the entire bay for such an encounter. Clearly hurt after the first strike, Cameron crawled back on to his board. He managed to paddle five metres towards shore before the shark seized him again. It dragged him and his board some 50 metres further out and began thrashing in a circular formation with such ferocity that a whirlpool formed. Cameron was tossed completely out of the water.

'There were fins, tails, blood everywhere. I don't want to talk about it too much,' Harry said.

After four minutes the water calmed. The shark and Cameron were gone. Some 200 metres further out, the back half of Cameron's surfboard popped up, as if spat out.

A ten-year-old boy ran through the car park, shouting a warning. Panic ensued. Who was the surfer? Grown men in wetsuits ran in circles. Finally, campers and locals twigged. A lady was screaming, inconsolable. The wife. The widow. So disrupted with shock was Tina Bayes, her legs became paralysed and she couldn't walk. An ambulance drove her to Ceduna Hospital, and from there she flew back to New Zealand.

TV cameras and newspapermen flooded into Cactus. A local nightmare! 'I had all the channels chasing me,' Harry tried to laugh. 'SBS, ABC, all sticking their cameras in my face. But I didn't really want to say anything, so I didn't.' He snorted. 'A lot of people who spoke to the media weren't even there. Ego comes into it.'

I heard the Bayes family were devastated when a South Australian newspaper ran a photo of the giant bite through Cameron's board, blank foam stained pink. I chose not to be a stranger shooting questions down the line to New Zealand, or to track down the local schoolchildren who'd witnessed the attack. I figured they'd been through enough already (a counsellor had been to the school).

And I was scared now too. Theories abounded. The shark was a rogue, injured, curious, territorial, gone to Elliston, a killer that must pay, still out there! Spring was dangerous: two previous attacks at Cactus had occurred in the same month but different years. Clifftop tourists at the Head of the Bight reported great whites devouring southern right whale afterbirth and attacking any sick or poorly guarded calves. Big sharks move inshore for seal calving too, and when the salmon pass!

The oceans are changing fast, being fished out, poisoned and slowly boiled. What do sharks think when fishermen dump fish-guts overboard, when humans in cages burley the water, when tuna are transported in massive mobile farms from the Bight to Port Lincoln, which stop every few days to allow the fish to be fed? Are the dumb sharks making connections?

Harry was speaking again. 'The worst is when there's no body left, no piece of wetsuit or even a fucking fingernail. You walk up and down the beach expecting to find something, though you never do.' Then came the news from Elliston. Harry shook his head. 'When we heard about the second attack, it was as though it was a mistake. The sequence was unbelievable really.'

An insect exploded on the Commodore's windscreen. I had just caused a random, violent death to a creature about which I felt only annoyance that its death-splat occurred right in the middle of my view of the road, meaning that I'd have to clean the 'screen at the next roadhouse.

I thought a lot about death on the 270 kilometre drive to Elliston on the western coastline of the Eyre Peninsula. There are many creatures that can kill humans in our wide brown land, from redbacks to death-rolling crocodiles. But you can kill the former with a single thong blow and at least climb a tree to escape the latter. Surfers generally accept that every creature has a place in the scheme of things; indeed, we are often at the front line of environmental rumbles. Yet who among us does not fear being eaten alive? My fear of the locals paled before this fear.

Jevan Wright was a regular visitor to Elliston. At 12.50pm on 25 September, Jevan rode his final wave to the end of Black's

Reef after a session with some mates and the father of his girlfriend. He was in the lagoon, only 30 metres from the jagged shore, when the great white hit. Two sudden, violent strikes, then ... nothing. A friend stood stunned on the reef. He could smell the fear, the blood, but there were no screams, no sign of Jevan. Just a shark — five or six metres long. Then it too was gone. Jevan's mate paddled out and retrieved the drifting front third of Jevan's surfboard. Freaking.

I turned into the dusty car park on a brilliant, mocking afternoon. The waves were good. I needed a surf desperately, so I leapt out of the car and clambered into my wetsuit. I stretched a bit, while hoping some other surfers might turn up, trying not to be transfixed by the small memorial that overlooked the lineup: a cairn of rocks, shells and a few West End cans topped with a simple wooden cross.

A car with two surfers turned up. 'Looks all right,' I said, trying to enthuse them.

'Maybe.' They drove off quickly.

I had believed that experiencing a little fear would help in my understanding of this story, but I never expected such intensity: the cliff climb ahead, the long lonely paddle, images of Jevan and Cameron, that cross ... My will snapped. I peeled off my wetsuit and stuffed it back into the board bag, where it would remain for the rest of my trip, and drove to Elliston to find a room.

The town was stunned. Grieving, angry, scared, confused, still searching. Shark sightings were the hottest news. There's one at Streaky, there're two big ones in Coffin Bay said a spotter plane, and a monster at Sheringa! Tales abounded of nets torn up and hooks straightened out, of researchers tagging more pointers in a single month than they normally would in a year. 'Cactus guys saw a mako breach and a school of bronzies!' said someone. It was the same killer shark!

One positive to emerge was how Elliston closed ranks after the attack. Within an hour there were ten boats out searching for Jevan, plus the SES from Streaky Bay and Port Lincoln, plus offers from other boats, even aeroplanes, all over the peninsula. 'Everyone pulled together,' beamed the lone local cop, Sergeant Allen Argent. Burly abalone diver Jeff Grocke was in a meeting at Lincoln when the news broke. He charged up the coast to join the search, which ran for four days. Nothing was found.

I spent an afternoon with Jeff watching too many shark documentaries and listening to too many shark stories. 'Great whites are extremely cunning and curious fish,' said Jeff, whose eighteen-year-old son Jethro surfs. 'They'll hide under the boat and generally not spend a lot of time on the surface where they can be seen.' Jeff believes there is now an overabundance of predators to prey; hence the predators are seeking new prey. The abalone industry is pushing for a cull, and Grocke is the man for the job. 'Scientists behind their desks,' Jeff spat. 'They don't believe what we say, they don't get out in the field. We've all been buzzed. No one in the abalone industry is working.' Jeff is also annoyed that if a fisherman accidentally kills a great white, he has to contact the Fisheries Department: 'It's like a murder inquest and you're supposed to feel guilty.' Scientists take the sharks away for testing and the fishermen receive no compensation, which hardly encourages cooperation. 'A dog bites someone, it gets shot. But a shark eats a kid, and the fishery blokes come out to check we haven't hurt any sharks! But you can guarantee 100 per cent the shark that took Jevan will be back.'

After days of talking and thinking only about sharks my fear was a tumour out of control and I was a human shark feeding on death, struggling to understand the fundamentally unknowable, to wring desperate meaning from a creature as far removed from notions of human morality as the world-devouring Galactus. I yearned to charge north to Ceduna Airport, to flee South Australia. Instead, I drove south toward Port Lincoln, a big town on Eyre's extremity made fat by the wealth of the ocean that surrounds it — south, that is, to a meeting with Jevan Wright's family.

I phoned Jeff Wright only because I'd heard he wanted to devote the rest of his life to ensuring that attacks such as the one on his son never happened again. Jeff met me at the door; his wife Katrina puffy-eyed in the background and Jevan's younger brother at school. I would soon learn much about the Wrights' remarkable son.

Jevan was taken a week before his eighteenth birthday and his coxswain's ticket exams that would have given him his first adult wage. 'So he didn't get to buy his first beer over the bar,' said Jeff, who'd only recently bought a mini-mal so he could get back into surfing with his two sons.

Beyond the kitchen window the sun broke through. I chuckled at a classic shot of Jevan in the local paper, with dreads and tank-top, shaking hands with a bloke from the council wearing suit and tie. It seemed that after two years of Jevan's lobbying, Port Lincoln Council had at last agreed to build a skate park for the local kids. No wonder Jevan's boss, skipper John McKenzie, declared: 'Jevan was a mighty man, I tell you, a man in his own right!' His name the Welsh for warrior, Jevan had a steady girl, worked hard and lived to surf and skate. No wonder over 400 people and a rock band turned up for his tribute service.

Jeff Wright knows the truth lies somewhere between shark hunter Vic Hislop and a shrieking media, who stir up fear and vengeance, and the scientific community, who seem sometimes more concerned with convincing us that sharks are basically just misunderstood. 'There seems to be little liaison between the scientists and bureaucracy and the divers and fishermen,' said Jeff. 'The old guys at sea can know a lot more than some young guy in an ivory tower who's never experienced the ocean.' Jeff wants to help make shark-repelling technology affordable for every surfer, to erect signs at beaches, shake up the world, do whatever it takes to make, of Jevan's death, something tangibly affirming. 'I'll push my barrow for as long as it takes,' he said quietly, and I believed him.

The Wright family were only weeks into a grieving process that would never end, coping in their own ways but still fragile. I compared my own petty emotions to what this open, inspiring couple endured every day — outliving their child — and felt ashamed. The Wrights let me into their lives for half a day and, in the process, changed mine. I hope they don't regret the experience.

Apart from the obvious risk of driving too fast in a rented Commodore, we don't confront death much in modern life. We muse on our own death even less. Few moderns kill their own meat or have any concept of the food chain, let alone of being a part of that chain. Death thoughts create fear. Yet if confronted, riding on adrenalin, fear can lead to ecstasy. Flirting with death is the unmentioned basis of surf stoke. This is why big waves are more exhilarating than small ones, why solo night sessions are such a buzz; why every session in South Australia is accompanied by an intense awareness of nature and the water movement around you that can border on either enlightenment or paranoia.

Surfers know, when surfing the Southern Ocean especially, that we are not the alpha animal, that death rides with the territory . . . not an ignoble death in bed, but death in the saddle, becoming one with the sea, white death. Death after being truly alive.

Rest in peace, Cameron and Jevan, and all the other 'statistics'.

First published in *Tracks* magazine, 2000.

7

WIND ON THE WATER

The frontier of surfing is always on
the move, from a Victorian beach, to a
Pacific crossing, to a Franciscan
church . . .

Jack Finlay

The swell had been weak for almost all of that year. People were
talking about fundamental shifts in the earth's weather systems.
The papers and the talkback radio shows had latched on to the
floods in January, the snows in February, the March heatwaves
and other extraordinary empiricals as some sort of evidence that
things were out of kilter. There was mention that the weather
had 'gone mad', but it never seriously worried me. I was happy
enough to take it as it came, and I knew it would come, it always
does, if not tomorrow then certainly the day after.

On the beach the sand swept through a semicircle, the tips of which ended in the ochre and dun coloured cliffs of sparsely vegetated headlands. Off both of them a swell was breaking, peeling down a half tide rock shelf in a desultory fashion. If you had asked me whether there were waves, I would have said, 'Yes, but only if you're desperate.' It wasn't what I would call surf. But the signs were there. The wind was back in the northwest and swell lines could be seen out at sea from the car park at the tip of the northern headland — faint and indistinct, almost like brush strokes of wind on the water.

The movement of the swell itself was a stippling. I've seen flocks of muttonbirds create this same effect when you disturb them on a calm sea. The flutter of the wings, the movement of the feet centimetres above the surface, and the sound, create a swirl of sensation, that sweeps across the water as the flock rises, then just as quickly fades and is lost. Well, this swell was something similar, patches of silent stippling coming forward, not in unbroken lines as it does when there is strength to it, but subtle and irregular, here and there. If you were surfing there would have been long waits between waves.

The sand of the beach had a strange light to it. The sun was just up but a cloudbank masked it. The effect was a golden grey, and the air had a restful feel to it, like a sigh during sex.

Down from the car park small groups of people had gathered and were carrying camera boxes and light reflectors on to the sand. It was some type of photo shoot. I nodded to one of the women in the group as I passed by. She was talking to the others, and I heard her use the term 'the frontier of surfing'.

It was mid-tide, and below the rubble of rock at the cliff base the beach sloped gently down to the water's edge. Every so often the surge of a wave would sweep up over the sand completely clearing it of markings and footprints, leaving a finely granulated surface, pristine and virginal.

As yet another wave performed this cleansing ritual a small fragment of something caught my eye. It had been deposited midway between the water and the rocks, and only stood out because of the smoothness of the sand.

At first I thought it was a pebble washed up or uncovered by the incessant movement of the water. Two or three steps from it I realised it was something else, a fragment of glass, no bigger than my thumbnail, silver green with sea age and smooth beyond comprehension.

I knew at once where it had come from. Barely half a kilometre across the beach from where I stood, the torn and rusted remains of a clipper ship lay scattered along the length of the reef that skirted the headland. Over the years I had dived and explored and sought out its relics of door handles, glass and china fragments, slate and rust-fused metal. That's where this little piece had come from, after a journey of a hundred years. I picked it up and put it in my pocket, my fingers sliding across its irregular smooth surface. Wave energy, I mused.

Captain Chapman had made a solitary small mistake. One

dark May night he mistook the lights of a coffee palace on the cliff tops for a lighthouse, and the waves did the rest.

Close to where his ship had grounded and broken up, a lone Malibu rider was now paddling out to try the left-hander that was breaking perhaps every six to eight minutes. Pretty slim pickings. Along the beach behind me, three figures had settled for the speed of the beach break.

Waves? What do any of us really know?

In 1872 the clipper ship *Loch Vennacher*, on passage from Glasgow to Melbourne on almost the same latitude as I now stood, but further west, encountered two huge seas. The first one she rode over, the second one towered over the boat and broke halfway up the masts, filling the lower topsails 60 feet (18 metres) above the deck.

Hundreds of tonnes of water swept over the ship, taking out its masts and washing the cook and his galley overboard. So violent was the shock, and so loud the shrieking of the wind, that none of the crew clinging to the poop deck heard the crash of breaking rigging as the masts came down.

In 1933 in the north Pacific, the American naval vessel USS *Ramapo* rode out a typhoon during which she encountered a wave of 110 feet (34 metres).

What do any of us really know? A bridgehead of sorts, a frontier if you like, has been opened up with tow-in surfing, but there's still a lot of virgin territory to be explored.

* * *

There is no real beginning to the process. It never started at a known date. Its origins are obscure, a mishmash of myth and scientific hyperbole. But somewhere in the eons of time, in the swirling of dust and cloud, a process was begun that has gone on for millions of years.

The component parts are many. The variables and combinations almost defy mathematical analysis. Hot air rises, cool air descends. The tilt and rotation of the earth and its orbit of the sun give rise to higher temperatures at the equator than at the poles, and a massive circulation of sorts begins.

A movement of air is deflected, pushed and drawn this way and that by the earth's geography, by pressure and temperature differences, hemispheres, solar flares, the heating of deserts and oceans, the heights and alignments of mountain ranges, coastlines, and the all-pervasive spin of the earth, the Coriolis effect which 'bends' the wind.

Westerly belts, subtropical convergences, jet streams, warm and cold fronts, cyclones and anti-cyclones, the list goes on but eventually it all relates to wind energy and open ocean swell.

In 1643 Evangelista Torricelli invented an instrument to measure atmospheric pressure; in time it became the barometer. In 1816, using Torricelli's invention, H.W. Brandes of the University of Breslau drew the first known isobaric weather chart and confirmed that weather sequences corresponded with giant atmospheric circulations of high and low pressures that moved around the earth.

The *Sydney Morning Herald* on 5 February 1877 published Australia's first weather map. It featured among its detail a low over southern New South Wales that was moving eastwards. I've sometimes wondered what effect that had as it moved out to sea.

In all this release of energy and its ocean potential, the one horrifying figure that stands like a beacon in my mind is the 187-knot (347-km/h) winds generated in the Gulf of Mexico in 1969 by Hurricane Camille.

I have often heard surfing described as a 'weather sensitive' activity.

There was no word for astronomer in the Gilbertese language. If you wished to find an expert on the stars you asked for a 'Tiaborau' or navigator, astronomy being looked upon only as an adjunct to the larger science of navigation.

Of the thirty thousand inhabitants on the Gilbert Islands in my time, less than twenty could speak with authority about the stars, and those who had the authority were often unwilling to pass it on, for of all the secrets, those connected with navigation were the most jealously guarded.

(*Arthur Grimble: Early Writings*)

We had finally left the river mid-morning on a Friday, after two days holed up waiting for the norwester to ease off. When we awoke that morning the wind was still shrieking through the masts of the fishing boats, and one of the fishermen, a character they called 'Slippery', said to me by way of warning when he knew we were leaving, 'Nothing fine ever came out of the northwest'.

The fishermen had stood on their boats watching as we motored upstream to turn around. Not one of them said a word. They stood there silently surrounded by their craypots and ropes and plastic floats and it was obvious what they thought.

At the river mouth I looked across to where the lighthouse stood, etched starkly white against the grey of the cloudbank to the south. A genuine ten-foot swell was sweeping round the point and peeling down the reef, its top being torn back by the wind. Not a surfer was out.

We hoisted a heavily reefed mainsail and a tiny jib and set off at breakneck speed down the coast. At that stage the slant of the wind was still offshore, but as we pulled out from under the headland that sheltered the river mouth, we began lifting to what the met bureau was calling a 'heavy swell'. The land to the north was partially obscured by rain squalls and appeared only at times as the drifts scudded through. At that stage the wind was probably around 30 knots with higher squalls.

The midday forecast carried gale warnings, grazier and sheep weather alerts, and a litany of other diabolical weather extremes. None of us said anything when we heard it. We were only thankful we were going with it. The barometer, which had been falling for nearly 24 hours, continued downwards.

In the early afternoon of that initial day, the first of the cold fronts swept in from the southwest just as Slippery had intimated they would. We gybed across to take the new slant it offered, but such was the force of the wind and the size of the swell that quickly built up with it, that even with the mainsail let out, the boat heeled so much the boom dragged dangerously in the water. We brought it in, dropped the sail and ran off under the jib alone. God, it was bleak.

By nightfall, as we passed the Cape and headed out to sea, a huge open ocean swell had risen, hailstones the size of fingernails were hitting the deck, the sea was a heaving mess of blown spume, and an albatross was calmly criss-crossing our wake.

In the early part of the night successive fronts swept across us, and we steered by the feel of the wind over our right shoulders and by the direction of the swell.

Around midnight the wind steadied to about 30 knots with gusts to 45 or 50, which is what it had been blowing for periods in the afternoon. A full moon would occasionally break through the cloud drift, illuminating the whole tumbling madness in a veil of ghostly white.

Standing at the wheel with 55 feet (17 metres) of yacht stretched out in front of me, the jib rock-solid with wind, the whole scene took on a surreal, dreamlike air, an unreality not unlike a video game.

The most unbelievable swells were passing under us. Sometimes their tops were breaking 'just over there' in great thundering rolling cascades of white water. Occasionally the noise would be astern and come down over us, hitting the yacht with a thump, sending up plumes of spray and filling the cockpit, leaving you gripping the wheel thigh-deep in water.

At other times the stern would slowly lift as the swell swept in, the yacht would rise, then at the top its bow would dip slowly, further and further, until the whole 12 tonnes of boat began a headlong rush at perhaps 20 knots down into the moonlit valley below. Surfing? I found out about surfing that night.

I thought of William Albert Robinson, a maritime wanderer and seeker of truth, and what he described as 'the culminating experience of a lifetime of voyaging'. Deep in the great southern sea his 21-metre, 50-tonne yacht *Varuna* had slid down the face of huge concave seas like a surfboard. 'When you have done that,' Robinson wrote, 'you have experienced something.'

Our course took us out even deeper into the ocean, and eventually northeast towards what had been called 'Pacifica'.

For us at that time it was still a myth of sorts, a concept if you like. The opening of Tavarua and the surf camps of the Pacific hadn't really touched us. In a sense we were still innocents and our trip had connotations of Melville and Stevenson, Jack London and Louis Becke. Not one of us gave a hoot about Kelly Slater or anyone else. Sure, they were surfers, but so were we.

The gale of the first night passed, and in retrospect was the hardest weather of our passage. If you have to cop these things then the best that can happen to you is that they pick you up early and that you're going the same way as they are. Over the entire duration of our passage we experienced a weather spectrum from gale to calm.

Each morning the sun would rise almost dead ahead, lifting from the sea as a bright golden orb on some mornings, while on others its energy and radiance would be hidden behind cloud banks from which shafts of light shot upwards and outwards.

At times we used natural phenomena to guide us. Swell and wind directions, cloud formations, bird life at sea, and of course always the stars. For nights on end we would pick a rising star and hold it for some hours against a known point of the rigging such as a crosstree or shroud, and then as it rose higher in its eternal traverse of the sky we'd move to another, lower star and repeat the process. In this way we might start the night with Altair fine off the bow, and finish it with Betelgeuse held on the starboard crosstree. Tahitians call this star path, or succession of rising and setting stars along which you steer, the 'Aveia'. Tongans call it the 'Kaveinga'.

With our sextants, charts and tables, and satellite navigation, we were of course dilettantes, players in the great sweep of voyaging. Our destination lay out there at some place with a set of known co-ordinates. Not for us the great unknown. After five days in the open ocean with no land, just 'the blue desert', I remembered the reaction of Caroline Islanders when first shown a magnetic compass by sixteenth-century Spanish explorers. When he realised the function of the compass, one of the Islanders pointed to a grey-haired old man standing on the beach and indicated that inside *his* head was *their* compass.

Whales, sharks, dolphins and seabirds crossed our tracks periodically. In the dark of night sometimes, dolphins would streak towards us like torpedoes, trailing great tails of luminescence behind them. On the third morning a humpback whale surfaced beside us barely ten metres away, and stayed there following us for the best part of an hour. His hide was scarred in long streaks with barnacles encrusted in lumps here and there.

The days and nights passed. The continuous motion of the boat at sea became our world, its slow progress the measure of our time. Our lives eventually left the land, severing to some extent even the emotional idea of land and home. Our universe was the yacht and the sea and sky around us. Food and sleep came to assume immense importance for each of us, and in this way we rolled from day into night into day, from one watch to another, from gale to calm, sunlight to rain, swell to swell.

Early on the morning of the tenth day, sometime around 2am, as I peered above the spray dodger to check the sea ahead, I caught the first smell of land. Perhaps it was pine needles, or grass, or just earth, but the aroma clearly reached my nostrils. It might not have been the scent of vanilla and musk that first greeted Conrad or Stevenson, but the effect was the same for me. It meant we were no longer alone out there, but more than that, for me it was another landfall at dawn.

We sighted the island soon after first light. A small indistinct dot in the grey haze of the horizon. As we worked our way in closer its features took definition: mountains, valleys, palm trees, a lighthouse and habitation.

Just before midday we passed through the opening in the reef of the atoll, west of the lighthouse. It was low tide and on either side the reef lay dried out and exposed. Off into the far distance, here and there lay a series of rusting broken hulks, fishing boats, yachts and island traders, all of which had somehow missed the entrance and ploughed up onto the coral.

As we passed through the reef the outgoing tide created a turbulence and where it met the brunt of the open ocean swells it caused them to stand up and the odd one was close to feathering. On either side of us, stretching off to left and right as far as the eye could see, eight- to ten-foot flawlessly formed waves were peeling left and right and running uninterrupted for hundreds of metres. There was no one out, there was no surf camp, and we appeared to be the only surfers there.

Standing on the deck, slowly making our way in past all this, I again heard someone use the phrase 'the frontier of surfing'. It was where we had arrived all right, but I wasn't too sure just then if that's the exact term I'd have used.

It was a warm summer's evening and Italy's Arno valley lay stretched out below us. Heapings of rain clouds hung heavily on the hills in the distance, offering a rare evening respite from the humidity of the day.

We were on an escarpment of some sort, and behind us a cobbled walkway fell steeply away to the main street of Fiesole. Pencil pines and old villas reached away in clusters along the ridgelines to our left and right. Directly under us a copse of olive trees clung to the slope that stretched down at an oblique angle to the countryside below.

The heat of the day had lost its edge, and as the sun dropped a light breeze lifted the haze and pollution of Florence so that the city with its domes and spires, and bridges and acres of red tiles, took on a clearer definition. For a time, here and there in the far distance below us, a window or a surface of some type would catch the golden light of the setting sun and send it back as a pinpoint of vibrant, intense luminescence.

As the day finally settled, and drew itself off the earth as a handkerchief is drawn from the pocket, a soft purple darkness slipped in to take its place. Slowly lights became visible, spreading through the valley in clusters and lines in all directions, until they gathered like a million dollars as far as the eye could see.

We were seated on a stone wall looking down on all this. There were four of us, Giannino, Annmaree, Laurene and myself. By one of those quirks of fate, or Karma, it was surfing that had brought me here, and the incongruity of it all was not lost on me.

Earlier that morning I had experienced one of my life's most profound moments. Jetlagged and footsore, I had stumbled into the Basilica of Santa Croce, a Franciscan church dating from the second half of the thirteenth century. Surrounded by 600-year-old frescoes, and the tombs of Renaissance figures such as Michelangelo and Machiavelli, I found myself in a small alcove to the lower left of the main altar.

A cluster of candles burned before a statue of the Virgin. Who had lit each one of these I wondered, and for what hopes did those flames flicker? From the corner of my right eye a movement caused me to half turn. There, in the gloom and grey of the vault that reached above the main altar, a single shaft of light hit a gold-embossed crucifix suspended perhaps four metres above the ground. In that precise instant, for the first time in my life, I understood with great clarity the basis of my own religious impulse, its relationship to the great sweep of human endeavour, and my long and fruitless search for peace, with its metaphor of the perfect wave.

Now, in the warm embrace of the night air, seated on a stone wall outside Fiesole, with its Etruscan tombs and amphitheatres, hundreds of kilometres from a wave of any sort, I faced again 'the frontier of surfing'.

Ostensibly we were talking about surf fashion (which is what indirectly had brought me to Florence) and its relationship to surfing itself. Giannino, who had never surfed in his life, used the term 'the *idea* of surfing' in describing how it was that the activity itself blurred at the edges and became something far bigger into which all people could reach for whatever it was they sought.

At one point I suddenly discovered we were discussing a memory of a group of Australian surfers and their 'DFA, the Dance of the Flaming Arseholes'. The discordance between the story and the surroundings didn't seem to matter. In fact it was better than that, they went together like whisky and water. Culture, time and geography, didn't amount to a hill of beans.

During all this, Annmaree made mention of a 'frontier of surfing'. I thought of how that phrase had come to me on a beach in Torquay, on the deck of a yacht in the western Pacific, and now on a hillside above Florence.

In its own way each of them captures something of the moveable feast that surfing is for me, the fact that it travels through time and place, from a wind blowing over the open ocean imparting its wave energy, to the deepest recesses of a mind pondering a shaft of light and a crucifix in a Florentine cathedral, or a piece of glass washed up on a beach.

When we left the hillside and made our way down the cobbled walkway to a restaurant with a vine-covered terrace, the frontier came with me, just as it always will. We dined on bean soup and drank Chianti. In the upper reaches of the Arno valley, somewhere out there in the night, a perfect wave stood up, feathered, then peeled off flawlessly along the edges of my mind.

First published in *Waves of the Sea: the ocean photography of Jon Frank*, Rip Curl, 1999.

8

BRUVVAS FROM THE GUTTER

On the mean streets of Maroubra it's important to know who your mates are

Matt Griggs

He wished he could do it all again. Just seconds earlier, the set of the day came through and Koby Abberton towed him into the perfect spot. The wave dropped suddenly below sea level, stepping, growing and contorting, only a metre or so from a dry ledge and into a barrel you could drive a truck through. It grew voraciously as it headed toward the channel where more 'Bra Boys, fresh from sending in two bodyboarders, were hooting from the boat. And then he did something no 'Bra Boy should do — he pulled back.

'You fucking dog! What the fuck are you doing? I'm never towing you into another wave for as long as I live,' Koby screamed at him as he manoeuvred his new four-stroke Yamaha Waverunner. On the side of his jet ski a sticker read, 'Ride with us or collide with us.'

'OK you've got one more chance,' Koby now called, as an even bigger set loomed. Koby waited till the slack was just right, then went full throttle, just about ripping the bloke's arms off. This time there was no pulling back and he dropped into the beast. 'Now fuck off!' yelled Abberton.

Koby only caught about eight waves all day himself (to the annoyance of the cameras in the channel), preferring to whip his mates into a few. 'To tell you the truth, I'm getting the biggest kick out of towing my boys. Half of 'em are footy players and have never experienced anything like this. My mate before, he can barely stand up and he got one of the best barrels I've ever seen. It made my day.'

Sydney Morning Herald, 24/12/02: At least 30 officers are now 'walking wounded' after a running brawl erupted between the gang [the 'Bra Boys] and off-duty police just before 1am on Saturday . . . Said one officer, who did not wish to be identified, 'The police copped an absolute flogging. They were outnumbered four to one . . . Some of the girls had their heads slammed into tables. A couple of blokes had their heads slammed into cars.'

Herald Sun, 24/12/02: . . . Four men were charged after the attack by members of the Maroubra gang, the 'Bra Boys, at the Coogee RSL Club on December 21, 2002. Randwick councillor Murray Matson said at the time of the attack there was anecdotal evidence to suggest the 'Bra Boys were running an extortion racket in Maroubra.

Daily Telegraph; 28/4/03: US-style gangs wearing coloured shirts and bandanas to identify their links have re-emerged across Sydney . . . Police have warned of growing instances of teenage thugs embarking on a campaign of fear, intimidation and, in some cases, violence not seen since the early '90s.

The *Telegraph* described the 'Bra Boys as, 'junior members of a senior crime gang in Maroubra, [with a] tattoo of "Bra" on the back of their neck.'

The incidents precipitated an onslaught of media attention which further reinforced the stereotype of the 'Bra Boys as a violent, organised and criminal group. Had the 'Bra Boys all turned to drugs, extortion, senseless violence and gang warfare? And shouldn't the tattoo say 'Bra Boys, not simply 'Bra? I went to Maroubra to find out.

It was Monday, and I figured I'd walk around before I met up with the boys after work. I started at the shops. There was a chemist, a bakery, a surf shop, a fruit shop, a fish and chip shop — and one café.

'Who? Who is 'Bra Boys?' The Asian shopkeeper had been in Maroubra eight months, and when I asked her about the people of Maroubra she replied, 'Good people, very good.'

I walked along the beach. The surf was small, but the grommets were all over it. The school holidays were in full swing. Just next to the neat, renovated surf club, there was a playground for toddlers and a skate park for teenagers. The place was alive with families. 'Yeah, I love it,' one kid wrapped in elbow and kneepads bigger than himself told me. I asked him if he'd seen anything scary happen in the area. He shrugged, looking up towards the car park where the 'Bra Boys hung out, then back to the skate ramp. 'Yeah, this guy tried a sick air once and fell on his head.'

'When I first joined the Boardriders I was only young,' said a local charger, Richie Vaculik, who met me in the car park. 'My mum used to come down and stay on the beach all day to watch me. But after she met all the older boys, she was stoked with how everyone was down here at the beach and totally trusted me with them. As long as I was with them, she was happy.' We were sitting on the hood of the car, watching the waves come through. What started as two of us soon snowballed into thirty. As the guys arrived they gripped each other's forearm, then slid into their unique handshakes.

The feeling of pride in the area is intense, and one of the proudest is 32-year-old Jimmy Olsen. We went back to his place on the beach. The youngest Abberton, Dakoda, now eleven, was playing with his little mates in the parking lot outside Jimmy's unit. It's where Jimmy, along with Sunny Abberton and their elders, used to teach the kids to box. It's something the grommets learnt so they could help defend the area constantly under attack by rival gangs. 'It was the academy, mate, the kids loved it,' Jimmy said. He'd also wrestle with them, pretending to spar until all the grommets took him down, jumping on his shoulders and rumbling his legs.

Jimmy's family seemed used to his mates being there. In fact the boys were treated as family themselves. Jimmy's wife cooked us some bread before jujitsu training that night (the 'Bra Boys' new passion) and we went through some family albums. But the photos weren't of his wife and child, they were of the 'Bra Boys. Jimmy smiled proudly at them the same way he did with his own family. There were also newspaper clippings of every one of his mates who'd made the news. There was plenty of surfing press for Sunny, Jai and Koby Abberton, of course, as well as Mark Mathews, Paul Moffat and Tony Seddon. But not everyone here surfs, and Jimmy seemed even more proud of his boxer mate Ronnie 'The Grouse' Reardon. And perhaps Ronnie's story sums up a part of Maroubra that's close to every local's heart.

'He's had a tough trot,' said Jimmy. 'He was in jail for quite a while, also alcohol abuse, drink driving, you name it — he's been there. A guy pushed him in the pub and Ronnie opened him up with a schooner glass. He just can't handle the alcohol, y'know. To see him back on track now, after seven years, off the piss and doing so well . . . it's unreal. Look how fit he looks.' We were watching a video of Ronnie's fight from the previous Friday. The 'Bra Boys were all at the venue to support him and you could see the tears in his eyes when he turned his back to his TKO'd opponent and acknowledged his brothers in their seats.

We're still in Jimmy's lounge room when Macario 'Macca' Desouza rocks up. Macca's an up-and-coming videographer who's put together a documentary on the 'Bra Boys. As we watch his film, the screen flashes to a scene at a Maroubra Boardriders Club contest. In the middle of the frame, handing out coloured singlets, is a smiling and responsible-looking redhead. His image blends with the redbrick units behind him as if a part of the town had got up and walked around. He is Sunny Abberton, the 'Mayor of Maroubra'.

Sunny's been at the forefront of everything, taking grommets down the coast, teaching them how to surf, box and get fit. He's been the father, mentor, captain, coach and superglue of the 'Bra Boys — and by extension, of Maroubra itself. Sunny, like so many people growing up in the local housing commission places, grew up with nothing. He was given surfboards, clothes, wetsuits and lifts down the coast by his elders. 'Maroubra is unique in a real tribal sense,' says Sunny. 'It's an area where everyone gets along. All of us — surfers, footy players, shopkeepers, the grommets — it's all one big family and it's had to be that way to survive.'

At a young age, Sunny was introduced to gang warfare. He was taught how to fight and defend his beach from rival gangs moving in from neighbouring suburbs. 'When we were growing up, we were doing war games behind the shooting range. That's how I grew up. We had to be ready, fit and strong, so as not to get chased out of town. We grew up with that danger hanging over our heads and that's what brought us all so close together. We went through some really heavy shit. Gangs were coming in from different areas and we were being trained and just getting ready.'

'The people of Maroubra have been known as the 'Bra Boys since the '60s, when surf culture first hit,' Sunny goes on. 'In the late '80s and early '90s, when that American gang culture came and the new housing commissions came, it brought a lot of kids from troubled spots towards the beach and surrounding suburbs, and gangs were formed. They traditionally hated surfers and they came down in organised gangs really wanting to take us on.'

While the rest of Sydney had a makeover and cleaned up its streets, that little country town on the edge of the city was forgotten about — and a battle was raging way beyond what was reported in the papers. This story — like the place itself, in a way — has been neglected for a long time.

'When I was growing up it was the bikies. These days it's the homeys coming from Redfern, Marrickville and places like that. The homies had come in without knowing the rules and without respect. I'm talking fifteen to twenty guys, armed, coming to the beach looking for surfers to beat up. We weren't going to stand for it.'

'We fought a bikie gang one time,' Sunny continues. 'Twenty guys who had come with baseball bats. We're talking big men. We were at a barbecue when we heard our mates going down. We came running out with poles and burning wood from the fire at the party and we fought, all armed, in the middle of the street. Then they pulled out guns and started shooting. We've seen some crazy stuff that you'd never hear of. Drive-bys were happening all the time at one stage [in the early '90s]. I've been at a party on the beach and someone's trying to run over one of the boys with a car. We've had our houses attacked — bricks and shit coming through the window, y'know, trying to get to us. They don't muck around. I've been hit with an axe in the leg. I don't want to name the gangs, but these Syrian gangs have come down with big knives and stabbed the boys. But we didn't lie down — and what happened to them afterwards was pretty serious. The ambulance guys who took them away said they had every bone in their body broken . . .

'We just grew up in an area where we had to bond together to be fit and push each other — to survive,' says Sunny. 'It's a hard thing to get caught up in, but when guys are running at you with guns and you see your younger brothers getting beat up, knifed and shot at, what do you do? Koby and that have had guns held at their head since they were thirteen, y'know. We solved a lot of those problems and we get along with them now. They've accepted our way — you know, 'Ride with us or collide with us' to use one of Koby's terms.'

* * *

City-style gentrification is slowly starting to reach Maroubra, but the trouble still lurks like a dark shadow. Therefore Sunny, Jimmy and the like have kept training the new generations, 'getting them ready'. 'We were young "houso" kids with nothing,' remembers Sunny. 'No money, no boards, no clothes. And still a lot of our kids are growing up that way, so we feel responsible for them. We expect all the older guys to as well. The young blokes still get grommet abuse, but only 'cause it means you get tested and pushed to make you a stronger and better person. It's been passed down to me and now you can see how we pushed Koby and see also how he's pushing Mark [Mathews], Evo [Evan Faulkes] and Richie [Vaculik] — you know, the new guys coming through.'

One of those coming through, rising star and charger, Mark Mathews, said he'd experienced a lot. 'All the drugs, violence, nightlife, the multiculturalism, the gangs. You really learn the value of friendship. A lot of the kids don't have family support and without the support from your mates, it's hard to keep your head up. There's no bullshit here. Just mateship and family above all else, pride in what you do and where you come from.'

Describing Maroubra came easily for Mark, especially after being on the road so much now. 'Picture the famous Bondi Beach. Can you see it? Now replace those shitty closeouts with consistent banks, get rid of 90 per cent of the tourist population, rub out all the fuckwit yuppies and install a hardened, down-to-earth family of locals. Then add a shitload more character and pride and you've got Maroubra!'

*   *   *

If there's a hero in the 'Bra now, it's Koby Abberton. 'Koby was the one we all wanted to make it,' Sunny said, of his younger brother. 'From the age of eleven we were pushing him into 12-foot waves at Voodoo. He took it on and that's a special thing.'

Though Koby Abberton is living the good life now (fast cars, new house and large salary), it hasn't changed him and how he is. 'Maroubra is everything to me. It's home, it's life ... everything I believe in.' Koby moved out of the drug-riddled housing commission places when he was just thirteen, forging an even stronger bond with his elder brothers and mates who, along with his grandma, took care of him. You see that in the way Koby takes care of his mates now. Clothes, surfboards and wetsuits — everything that comes easily to Koby — gets passed on just as easily to his less fortunate friends.

The fact Koby's been one of the most publicised surfers in recent years has given others a glimpse into the life of the 'Bra Boys, though the 'Ride with us or collide with us' attitude has often overshadowed his true philosophy. 'My whole life is about my family, my mates, and doing it the hard way, that's pretty much it.'

Koby recently celebrated his outlook on life by acquiring a tattoo across his chest that reads: 'My Brothers' Keeper.' 'It just means I'll look after my brothers till the day I die,' he said.

That weekend, I joined Koby and the rest of the 'Bra Boys in supporting their local footy team, the Coogee Wombats. A new little charger, the outside centre David Skene, was carrying on the tradition the 'Bra Boys have fought so hard to protect. 'You don't have to be a good surfer here, or good anything,' Koby said proudly. 'Whatever it is that you're doing, you just have to *charge*.'

'And if you don't?' I asked.

'You take a back seat your whole life.'

First published in *Tracks* magazine, 2003.

9

THE SURF OF THE CHIEFESS

Approaching forty, with a young child,
one woman realises it's now or never for
her teenage surfing dreams

Fiona Capp

In Nevil Shute's apocalyptic 1957 novel *On the Beach*, Melbourne is the last place on earth untouched by nuclear war. The film adaptation starring Gregory Peck and Ava Gardner opens and closes with the image of an American submarine passing through The Rip at Port Phillip Heads like one of the last great dinosaurs of the sea. The submarine has fled to Melbourne because there is nowhere else to go. Popular myth has it that, during the filming, Ava Gardner quipped that Melbourne was a perfect place to make a movie about the end of the world. The quip was, in fact, the invention of a Melbourne journalist.

Like many Australians, I grew up thinking about Australia in this apocalyptic light, as somewhere stuck away at the bottom of the world; where everyone was used to making pilgrimages to Europe as though that were the centre of civilisation. Then, in my late thirties, I returned to surfing after a fifteen-year break and began an odyssey that took me to Hawaii, Cornwall and the southwest coast of France. By the time I got back home, I realised that the world would never again look quite the same.

Although I had given up surfing in my mid-twenties, soon after I'd started work as a journalist, I could never throw off the feeling that I was only half alive when I was away from the sea. Waves loomed in my dreams. I'd wake before being engulfed, but strangely I didn't wake in fright. I was left, as always after dreaming about the sea, with a residue of hope and longing. Occasionally, when the subject of surfing came up in conversation, I would remark that I still had my wetsuit and board and that I intended at some stage to return to the water. But eventually the claim started to sound wishful and even hollow: an expression of nostalgia rather than genuine intent. I lived in the inner suburbs of Melbourne a hundred kilometres from the surf, and now had a young child; life had settled into a comfortable routine. And yet, when sitting in the local park watching the other parents playing with their children, I would be gripped by a quiet feeling of panic. During holidays as I swam in the shorebreak at Sorrento back beach — near Port Phillip Heads — and played with my baby boy in the rock pools, I would find myself casting furtive glances toward the surfers out beyond the break, like Prufrock watching the mermaids riding seaward on the waves and wondering, 'Do I dare?' If I didn't make a move to join them soon, I feared I never would.

For many years I'd found a million good reasons why I couldn't take up surfing again. Then one wintry day, when the novel that I had been wrestling with for months finally ground to a painful halt, I saw all my good reasons for what they were. A week later, I was in the car heading down to the family beach house at Sorrento to see if I could still squeeze into my old surfing skin, the wetsuit I had not worn for so long. It hung on a hook in the corrugated iron sleepout along with all the old beach paraphernalia — buckets, beach balls, kickboards, bodyboards, hula hoops, deck chairs and badminton shuttles. I lifted the wetsuit off the hook fully expecting it to fall apart in my hands. Gingerly I turned it in the right way, arm by arm, leg by leg, looking for spiders. From one leg gushed a handful of sand and I wondered what beach it was from — the beach of my last surf.

Above all other obstacles, it was fear that had held me back in surfing and, later, kept me out of the water. Fear of failure, fear of being an impostor, fear of being out of control. All these fears coalesced in the tell-tale corrugations of a big set looming out the back, that unstoppable phalanx of pure, liquid energy from which there was no escape. It was my hope that this time I could begin to overcome the more debilitating aspects of this fear. And yet perversely, a certain aspect of it — the awe I felt in the presence of this natural force, a force so unfathomable that it grants you an inkling of infinity — was intrinsic to my attraction to surfing. In Wordsworth's description of his younger self bounding over the mountains and the lonely streams of the Wye River valley 'more like a man/ Flying from something that he dreads than one/ Who sought the thing he loved', I saw myself out in the surf.

Yet I knew that my love of the sea was not just about the attraction of the sublime. Most surfers talk openly about the sheer joy of *being in the water*. Informing this understatement is a philosophy — sometimes couched in spiritual terms — about connecting with a force vastly greater than oneself, about returning to 'the source'. It harks back to a sensation invoked by the French writer Romain Rolland in his metaphor 'the oceanic feeling'. Rolland used this phrase when writing to Freud about an essay of Freud's that treats religion as an illusion. He agreed with the psychoanalyst's views on religion but felt that Freud had not appreciated the true origin of religious sentiments. Such sentiments were borne, Rolland said, of a feeling which was always with him and which others too had confirmed; a feeling which he described as a sensation of eternity, of something boundless or oceanic.

Freud could not find this oceanic feeling in himself and did not regard it as the origin of religious belief. But he did concede that it may be a residual memory of that earliest phase of psychic life when the child and the world are one. Few images better capture this primal 'at-oneness' than that of the surfer crouched inside the crystal, womb-like tube of a breaking wave; an image made all the more exquisite by our knowledge of the wave's imminent destruction. No sooner has the surfer returned to that all-embracing amniotic realm than she is unceremoniously expelled into the harsh light of the world. In fact, this birth analogy is built into the Hawaiian word for surfing, *he'e nalu* — 'wave sliding'. The first part *he'e* means 'to run as a liquid' or 'to flee through fear', while the second refers to the surging motion of a wave or the slimy liquid on a newborn child.

Cautiously I eased the wetsuit on. Apart from a tear at the base of the right leg, it remained in one piece. The cool rubber encasing my body felt strangely familiar. I pulled up the zip and went to look at myself in the mirror. I grinned at my reflection. Fifteen years seemed to fall away. Flinging open the back door, I leapt down the steps and did cartwheels across the lawn.

Most of the waves that break on the shores of southern Australia have been generated by low pressure systems in the high latitudes of the Indian and Southern oceans, close to Antarctica. Coasts in the southern hemisphere are, as Rachel Carson puts it, 'washed by waves that have come from lonely, unvisited parts of the ocean, seldom crossed by vessels, off the normal routes of the airlines.' My waves came from the deep south but my cultural ties bound me to the north. An abiding sense that Europe lay on the other side of the horizon had always complicated my feelings about surfing. As a young woman, I felt that my two touchstones — surfing culture and European culture — belonged to separate, incompatible universes. Modern surfing, as opposed to the ancient Hawaiian art, was a New World, not an Old World, phenomenon. Not long after returning to surfing, I dreamt I was standing in front of the Doges' Palace in Venice looking towards the white dome of Santa Maria della Salute, when I noticed some surfers in the water. Without warning, a perfect, glassy wave began rising slowly out of the lagoon like some mythical beast and I knew I had to get out there. Typically, I woke up before I had the chance to set foot in the water. But I was now determined to include Europe in my surfing odyssey in the hope of closing the gap between my two worlds.

Along with this personal compulsion to bring Europe into the equation was the compelling history of surfing itself. The first image of surfing made by Europeans is a watercolour by John Webber, the official artist on Captain Cook's third voyage to the Pacific, titled 'A View of Kealakekua Bay'. It depicts Cook's triumphant arrival on the island of Hawaii in January 1779. Double and single canoes full of Hawaiians crowd the water around the ships *Resolution* and *Discovery*. In the middle foreground a small figure paddles a surfboard over the choppy water toward the ships, and near the shore, another is pushing a surfboard out through waves. Along with Cook's journal entries, the painting records the moment when surfing entered European consciousness.

While surfing had been practised throughout the Pacific for thousands of years, in Hawaii it reached an unrivalled level of sophistication. The songs and *meles* or chants through which Hawaiian history and traditions were transmitted were full of stories about surfing romances, surfing gods, great surfing exploits and other surf-related dramas. Surfing was inseparable from the religious, sexual and social rituals of traditional Hawaiian life. My knowledge of this history was sketchy when I first set eyes on Webber's painting. But I sensed how big the story of surfing was; how surfing as a sport and as an emblem of ancient Polynesian society was caught up in one of the most significant moments in world history ... the moment when Enlightenment Europe stumbled on what it believed to be earthly 'paradise' — only to devastate it.

One day during his third voyage, Cook was out walking at Matavai Point in Tahiti, where he and his men were camped, when a man in a canoe caught his eye. The islander was looking about with an eagerness that Cook regarded as suspicious. At first he thought the man had stolen something from one of the ships and was being pursued. Then he realised that the islander was in fact absorbed in catching waves, and was totally uninterested in the Europeans' ships and tents close by.

He went out far from the shore, till he was near the place where the swell begins to take rise; and, watching its first motion very attentively, paddled before it, with great quickness, till he found that it overtook him, and had acquired sufficient force to carry his canoe before it, without passing underneath. He then sat motionless and was carried along, at the same swift rate as the wave, till it landed him upon the beach. I could not help concluding that this man felt the most supreme pleasure while he was driven on so fast and so smoothly by the sea, especially as, though the tents and ships were so near, he did not seem in the least to envy or even to take any notice of the crowds of his countrymen collected to view them as objects which were rare and curious.

(*Cook's Voyages*, Vol. II Chapter IX)

It's one of a number of episodes that reveal Cook's extraordinary appreciation of surfing's power to consume and excite one's whole being to the exclusion of all else. The Tahitian surfer's world was soon to be turned upside down by contact with the West, yet this surfer was neither beguiled nor distracted by the trappings of European civilisation. At that particular moment, he was a picture of self-contained serenity — surfing was all that mattered.

When Cook's journal and Webber's drawings were first published in Europe in 1784, they created a sensation. Here were Jean-Jacques Rousseau's 'noble savages'. Here was a southern Arcadia, the Utopia that Europeans had thought existed only in their imaginations; an ideal society free of hypocrisy, toil and sexual inhibition. Here was an 'ocean of desire' — as Bernard Smith puts it in *Imagining the Pacific* — in which all the nations of Europe would come to wallow.

Yet it was on this third voyage that Cook became painfully aware that his grand role as Enlightenment man was riven with contradictions, says Smith. 'Cook increasingly realised that wherever he went he was spreading the curses much more liberally than the benefits of European civilisation.' Hence his obsession with being portrayed by Webber as the great Pacific peacemaker. To modern eyes, though, Webber's painting of Cook's arrival in Hawaii looks more ominous than triumphant. Hindsight has given it the appearance of Eden at the moment of the Fall, with surfing a nostalgic emblem of man living in perfect harmony with nature — a harmony about to be shattered by the forces of civilisation.

In *Civilisation and its Discontents*, Freud turns this argument on its head when he blames the 'voyages of discovery' for much of the Western world's discontent with civilisation. These voyages, he says, encouraged the mistaken belief that native peoples were 'leading a simple, happy life with few wants, a life such as was unattainable by their visitors with their superior civilisation'. For Freud, humanity's struggle for happiness is a tug of war between the desire for individual freedom — which springs from that part of ourselves untamed by civilisation — and the necessarily restrictive demands of society. In Freud's history of civilisation, there is no period in which man cosily cohabitates with nature, no lost idyll. Nature is man's greatest adversary, a force to be feared or tamed. Civilisation — as symbolised by great European cities such as Rome — has been driven by the struggle for self-preservation in the face of nature's 'crushingly superior' forces. 'The elements seem to mock all human efforts to control their lives: the earth, which quakes and is torn apart and buries all human life and its works; water which deluges and drowns everything in a turmoil; storms which blow everything before them.' Civilisation is humankind's bulwark, making the renunciation of our most basic instincts the necessary price.

What Freud doesn't address — but what early explorers like Cook seemed to intuit — is how the repressed element of our psyches might find *release* in these potentially threatening forces of nature, just as it does in sex. This was how I had always understood surfing. And yet my dream of a perfect wave looming up out of the murky waters of the Venice lagoon seemed to endorse Freud's logic. Few symbols of Western civilisation better embody its fragility and artifice, its ongoing struggle for mastery over the natural world, than does Venice. A wave such as I had imagined would spell the destruction of this fairytale city built upon a collection of swampy islands and forever threatened by the encroaching sea. If this dream was any indication, my unconscious fear was that I could only have one or the other: Venice or the wave.

For a couple of years, surfing took me inexorably northward. I went to Byron Bay and then to Hawaii where I discovered, in the archives of the Bishop Museum of Polynesian Culture, Hawaiian chants — extraordinary epic poems and creation myths about the first gods surfing from island to island while lightning split the sky. I read surf chants dedicated to the likes of Queen Emma, widow of Kamehameha IV and friend of Queen Victoria — 'Red hot is the "surf" of the chiefess' — and to her rival King Kalakaua, whose chant describes him 'The chief whose waves obey his will'. The mere idea of Queen Victoria surfing is an amusing one (a cartoonist could have a ball with it), yet for Hawaiians there was nothing strange or laughable about a royal figure like Queen Emma surfing. To realise this is to begin to appreciate what surfing meant in Hawaii. That it could be political, physical, spiritual; that it had been integral to Hawaiian society in a way that it could no longer be in the modern world.

Although I had been to Britain several times before I arrived in Cornwall on the final leg of my surfing journey, I had never seen the coast. As I travelled, I turned to Virginia Woolf, who had spent her childhood holidays in St Ives and in whose books the sound of breaking waves can often be heard. 'Now we draw near the centre of the civilised world,' thinks Neville, the 'colonial' of the group of friends in Woolf's novel *The Waves*. 'The huge uproar is in my ears. It sounds and resounds under this glass roof like the surge of the sea. We are cast down on the platform with our hand bags. We are whirled asunder. My sense of self almost perishes. I become drawn in, tossed down, thrown sky-high.' It intrigued me the way the drama of the surf is used to register the impact of civilisation on a boy from Brisbane. Probably only a writer whose nation sang of 'ruling the waves' could do it.

Would I find here, then, on the British or French coast, that elusive blend of history, culture and nature that I had been searching for? Not surprisingly, perhaps, what I found forced me to reflect on where I had come from. In Biarritz I met a French surfer who spoke of French Polynesia as being 'empty' and remote from the modern world. It was language eerily reminiscent of the *terra nullius* concept of Australia held by early Europeans. The French, like the British surfers I had met, still regarded the Pacific as something of a colonial playground: the 'ocean of desire' that Bougainville and Cook created with their tales of the South Seas. At the same time they were acutely conscious that, in surfing terms, they lived on the world's outer edge.

On the long flight home, it began to dawn on me that the world looked different when you saw it through the eyes of a surfer. Intellectually I had known that Oceania was where surfing began and that it remained the centre of the surfing world, but these facts did not register in a personal way until I looked back on the Pacific from Europe's distance, and was freed from Europe's thrall. And now when I thought of the Pacific, I felt strangely possessive. The region in which I lived was defined not by land but by sea. Perhaps that was what my Venice dream had been all about. Somewhere between Orwell's nightmarish Oceania and Melville's divine Pacific that 'makes all coasts one bay to it; [that] seems the tide-beating heart of earth', I had found my home.

Based on the memoir *That Oceanic Feeling*, Allen and Unwin, 2003.

10

DOWN AND OUT IN LONDON

For a surfer, the cosmopolitan charms of the old country are lost in the throes of surf deprivation

Jimmy O'Keefe

Woken at ten, but not by an alarm. It's not a sweet sound either but a dirge, an organ or something. It black-clouds its way into the dingy cubicle I now call my bedroom and my ears prick and follow the sound.

Past the cat's piss on my windowsill, past the fillets of sweaty sole in the fish shop downstairs, and past the eternal whirlwind of rubbish that swirls around in our courtyard: a dust fountain tossing up yoghurt containers and cornchip packets like a fireman's blanket at a '50s beach party.

The sound gets louder as my ears exit the corrugated iron hatch that joins our house to the high street. Cleopatra's brothel is two doors up, but it's a fair bet the sound's not coming from there at this time of day. Beyond the Pakistani fruit vendor with his cardboard box full of sloppy black bananas and across the road and there's the culprit . . . the Gospel Church.

'That's the third funeral this month, I reckon,' my girlfriend says, spilling cereal on her bathrobe. 'Gang losers!'

I wonder if I'd seen him before. Was it 'T-Bo' the one-handed Jamaican yardie, always scowling, with a boombox under his good arm attacking passers-by with a speed-garage barrage? Or maybe it was one of the fifteen-year-old LA tryhards, clad in bandanas and do-rags who look at me funny every time I walk past the ringless basketball court. Could even be one of the Nigerian herb entrepreneurs who bop up the street in their black Mercedes Kompressor three or four times a day.

As I pack my backpack, the smell of neoprene and wax momentarily drowns out the sound of the organ, but the death music wins out. Supreme pensmiths Martin Amis and Saul Bellow describe death as invisible yet always there, like the thin black backing of a mirror — without which we wouldn't be able to see ourselves and make necessary decisions and adjustments to our lives.

As I make my way to the Tube station, surfboard under arm, I pass the church and, yep, the black Kompressor is parked not far from the hearse. A sea of people stand on the footpath, a couple of old ladies dressed to the nines and a couple of serious men in serious suits giving serious handshakes, but there's no wailing or tears for the departed.

Maybe it's because the corpse's fate is better than the rest of ours. He might be rotting in a wooden box, but at least he's in there by himself. For the rest of the neighbourhood — and indeed most of this cosmopolitan city — life is all about buildings stacked on top of each other, packed to the rafters with people; shitting, fighting, swearing, sexing and sweating. Numb, and all waiting to die, but filling in their time by creating as much noise and rubbish as possible.

If you need any more proof that humans are animals, come visit this little neck of the woods and its mausoleums for the undead. It looks like a reasonably OK city was picked up by a helicopter, lifted high and then dropped upside down, with human cockroaches rushing in to inhabit the ratholes. This is London.

Five hours, three train rides and a hire car later there's three of us tea-bagging in a howling onshore, so strong I'm sure it has blown the steep, green-haired cliffs a few metres inland. It's hard to believe I'm in the same country. It's five-foot waves and so onshore the faces are almost clean.

My first wave in three months pushes me to the bottom with no shortage of Atlantic power. It stretches my limbs like a dungeon rack, pulling my sagging muscles every which way and almost to breaking point. I come up in time for a quick breath and attempt to vomit the beef and Stilton Cornish pastie and can of Foster's I had for lunch. But there's no time, I'm back down on the bottom, stuck like a starfish to the Porthleven reef.

When I finally surface and gasp for air, I'm alive and smiling for the first time in weeks. A full body smile. It's like I've been pinned down and had a funnel jammed in my mouth and my innards filled with something the same glowing, atomic blue-green colour as radiator coolant, flushing my ulcerated stomach and dusty brain with jolting electricity.

Soon after, I'm sitting in the car, fumbling for the heater and trembling like a bus aerial in a too small carwash. I look in the rear-view mirror and make a decision. I'm a long way from the gangs of Cricklewood and Brent Cross, a long way from the dust fountain, a long way from Cleopatra's and a long way from the syphilitic cat that pisses on my windowsill, and it's gonna stay that way.

I'm not going back to that shithole.

First published in *Australian Longboarding*, 2001.

11

FAT CITY

The life and times of a surfing legend

Jack Finlay

Even now, after all this time, I find it hard to write about Jacky Paradise and those last final days down on the coast. Some things I can remember as if they happened yesterday. But others are only a stirring, a shiver if you like, a remembrance caught up in the debris of my mind.

Where these things ever start I don't know. At the time he was up north somewhere, maybe it was Mareeba or Moree. Who knows? He was flat broke and I sent him a few dollars for the fare down. There was a scabies outbreak in the Aboriginal section of

town and the southern press was having a field day with it. Even
without that I never thought it would all happen the way it did.
One of my old girlfriends used to talk about destiny, and perhaps
that's what this really was, a dark wind that was always going to
come in one day.

Jacky was quite amazing really. He was like a spirit that lived off
the land. It was as if he never needed food or drink as you and I do,
but drew his nourishment from everything that was about him
wherever he was. One moment it was dust and the long ever-
shimmering road, railway camps, empty wine flagons, fights and the
shrill screams of frightened women. Then it was something else.

I don't think it mattered to him where he was. All places
were the same. Two days after my call he was at the station. Just
like that. How he did it I'll never know.

I'd waited for him on a seat down by the ticket box at the end
of the platform. For a time I thought he hadn't made it. A lot of
people had walked past me and I was near ready to give it away
when up by the pedestrian footbridge that arches the tracks with
its soot-stained wrought iron I saw him. A small black man with
a pencil-thin moustache and a grey felt hat, carrying a suitcase
and a hessian sack of snakes.

I knew then I hadn't made a mistake. He was my man. The
pros might arrive in town in their hire cars, boards, baggage,
logos and all that paraphernalia stacked above them. But not
Jacky. He had some dignity and style. Jacky was never plastic.

I have to admit that at that time I hadn't been to a single
surfing contest in a long, long time. My feelings were more like

those of a Merle Haggard song. It was like looking at life through a frosted windowpane, a type of trouble in mind. I sort of had this hope that Jacky would wipe the window clean and things would be clear again like they used to be.

Fifteen years before this I'd been with him up north, boxing in his gym down by the old Manhattan Hotel. But I never thought things would work out the way they did. Even up to the moment he stepped off the rattler that autumn morning, I still believed there was a place for change in surfing. I never realised how far out of the mainstream I'd drifted.

On the Wednesday night before the surf contest I'd rerun that scratchy old '50s film of him in his first main event in the ring. He was only nineteen, and god he was good. Left hand, right hand, coming or going he could put you down just like that. Jab, hook, bob, weave, Jacky had all the moves. For a while there, a bit later, they started putting him in with some classy overseas imports and he still looked good.

When you're a black man and you've boxed, there aren't too many people you trust. They say it's best to travel light, and that's the way he always did it. That's how he arrived in town the day they started the surf contest. A small black man with a suitcase, a sack of snakes and a felt hat.

He told me once that early in his career he'd railed down south for a preliminary fight, and they'd tried to set him up. 'Those big stations are lonely places on a Monday morning,' he said, 'city noise, white tiles, wine bottles and brown paper bags.' He'd stayed at an old YMCA, with its all pervading stench of disinfectant, and the incessant coughing that came from behind almost every door.

They told him they'd arrange the corner for him. 'We'll save you a few quid, son,' they said, 'no need to bring anybody down with you, we'll put one of the best local trainers in your corner.' When three of the preliminaries fell short they rescheduled him for ten rounds. It took him just three of those rounds to realise his corner had their money on the other boy. It made no difference. When he won in the fourth they didn't like it. They told him he was finished. 'You won't be used down here again, mate,' they said, which proved to be incorrect.

Nothing had changed the morning I picked him up. All the booze and the shit jobs didn't matter, I knew he could still make the moves if he had to. His eyes were just as I'd always remembered them. Soft and dark and deep. Time and tent fights hadn't dimmed them one iota.

On that night that I'd watched the film of Jacky's epic bout, a depression had deepened in the high latitudes of the Southern Ocean. Its early movements went uncharted, but its centre was later registered at 998 hectopascals. Sure, the winds near its centre were strong, but its main influence on my life was felt when it tightened up the pressure gradients on the preceding high.

Around the time I'd arrived at the station the synoptic chart showed long westerly lines laid out like furrows in a wheat field. They began the contest that same morning in surf the media described as 'historic'. At the time I wondered what they meant, but it became clear soon enough.

By the time Jacky and I reached the beach a big swell was rolling. Big? I would say ten foot with much bigger sets. At that stage they were coming in rows of three or four every six minutes, and some of the pros were having trouble getting out. In fact just as we stepped down on to the beach a figure materialised on the sand beside us. It was one of the Americans. He'd tried twice and hadn't been able to clear the rocks. He was tired, just back from the brink of drowning and strung out. By the time he'd walked down the beach to below the flags and the judging stands his anger had him.

Barely ten metres from us he dramatically flung his board on to the sand, and looking over our heads at the crowd on the clifftop above he screamed, 'You motherfuckers . . . you sons of bitches . . . whadda ya mean sending us out in that . . . you bastards.' I don't know if it was directed at the judges or the crowd, but it made no difference. A few people laughed and that was it.

Jacky and I passed up along the beach beside the windmill, to where the old creek had once flowed. On the southern side there was a coarse gravel mound, and above it a bent ti-tree cut the skyline. Jacky still had his suitcase and the sack with the snakes. He looked terribly out of place. I wasn't beside him when he started talking so I don't really know how it all began.

Actually I was staring out to sea to where an albatross, a fully mature Wanderer, was rising and falling in a long lonesome glide above the swells at the horizon's edge. They aren't a common sight so close to land just here, and when I turned to tell Jacky I realised that he was a little distance off, standing on the incline of the gravel mound talking, and what's more that people were listening. Not only that, the group was quickly swelling as others pressed forward to hear what he was saying.

Style dictates some things, and it is probably better now if I don't even attempt to précis what he said. I guess the gist of it was what's described in the popular press as 'the notion of freedom', or 'liberation', or 'discovering one's way'. But those terms hardly do it justice. It centred strongly on individual responsibility, making up your own mind about things, and certainly wasn't anything even vaguely related to what the church hierarchies, and other social agencies, put forward. But I think that's how most people still see it, as a serpent to be ground under heel.

At about the point that Jacky first used the word 'salvation', or maybe it was 'freedom', I'm not quite sure, The Businessman drew me aside. He'd seen the crowd gathering and had come down to investigate. 'Salvation' wasn't a word he felt very comfortable about, even though Jacky's use of it had nothing at all to do with the notion of sin, as promulgated by the churches.

'Isn't this bullshit?' he said by way of an opening.

'Not at all,' I replied. 'You of all people should know that revival meetings don't happen down here.' I tried to personalise it by emphasising the 'you', hoping that somehow he'd take it on board, even file it away and maybe get to it later. It was always difficult trying to talk to him, to pin him down.

'There's a bit more to this than meets the eye,' I eventually added.

'I'll bet there is,' he said. 'Why the hell did you set this thing up? We're the only ones who know what's cool, and this isn't. What were you hoping to achieve?'

I looked at him. 'It isn't a set-up. It was always going to happen,' I said. 'Being cool is like trying to dam up water.'

I heard him mutter 'Oh fuck' under his breath as he looked away. Then he turned back and his voice was suddenly very strong and clear, but not loud. 'As far as we're concerned down here,' he said, 'the government's tax package is bullshit. Companies with loads of debt or heavy overseas borrowings are likely to find their interest rates eating into profits. Sure, you can hedge, but increased liquidity's the thing. Don't fall for the two card trick of rising costs and falling sales, and above all don't be blinded by conventional wisdom.'

At that time I didn't actually know what he was talking about — I was still just a surfer, at least in my own mind. But there was worse to come. He paused and his eyes ran out across the beach and along the line of the clifftop crowded with people. 'The economic reality is that the dollar is volatile,' he said. 'If I put so much as one foot wrong now, I'm a dinosaur in the economic desert. All this gone. I can wave Wall Street goodbye.' His hands gestured in a general sweep, and then he said, 'Real interest rates are here to stay. Get yourself a good tax accountant and a condo in Tahiti. That's the reality of surfing these days, not this . . . this . . . "freedom" bullshit.'

In retrospect, I think the length of the statement exhausted him. He wasn't given to sharing his thoughts with too many people, and even at the time I knew that in some sense I was being given as good a piece of him as it was possible to get. Earlier that same morning I'd seen him watching the waves through a pair of binoculars. He'd told me then that his main concern in life now was not how to make the drop on to another wave face, but only to find sufficient space on his T-shirts for another logo. He'd started to babble about 'branding' or something, but it sounded like mutton dressed up as lamb to me. 'This cotton polyester is wonderful stuff,' he'd said, 'a man could get involved with it in a personal way.'

Strangely, just two months after all this he went into receivership. His creditors had pulled the pin, and one of them was talking about possible 'tissue damage'. Under the circumstances, calling in the receivers was probably the best option for everyone.

Late in my dialogue with him, at almost the same instant he spat out the term 'freedom bullshit', a gasp went up from the crowd nearby. I knew what it meant. I'd heard it too many times before not to know, and in the early days I'd heard it slide from my own mouth. It meant Jacky had the snakes out.

I don't know if you've ever seen what happens to a crowd when the snakes come out. All those years of unfaced fears, forgotten childhood stories nurtured in the backblocks of the mind, the horror, the pale dry-mouthed clamminess, and the nervous bravado — well, it all comes together. The crowd gets restless, it falls back from the front like a wheat field before the wind, and sways with an almost sexual movement. Screams, and laughter devoid of any real substance, wash back and forth in a surge of fear. That's how it happened that morning at the back of the beach.

The first place I'd ever seen it had been one time when Ram Chandra performed in Townsville. But that performance had been entertainment pure and simple. This was different. This came in from the desert like a summer storm, in from the eons of time, from the genetic implanting at the dawn of man. It touched on the inner fear that lies in all of us, the one we always carry and contact sometimes in the early hours of the morning. Spooky and best left undisturbed.

I now found myself not knowing whether to look at Jacky, his arms festooned with snakes, writhing and alive, held up as if to shelter his face from the sun, or at the disbelieving group that stood around him.

The surfing had long ceased to matter. I no longer knew what was going on. There were ten-foot swells and they were sending out heat after heat. All I remember now is coloured singlets, jerky movements and a droning commentary that ran on and on in the background.

When I looked around to see how The Businessman was handling all this I realised he'd gone, faded off in to the background like a vapour. The people around me were total strangers and I looked everywhere for a familiar face. It was some time before I caught sight of The Kid. He'd changed, of course, but sure as eggs it was him all right ... Sitting in a director's chair at the edge of the cliff.

I'd last seen him the same year he won all those contests and I'd never forgotten the speed he could generate on a wave face. For a while there he was unbeatable and the press acknowledged that he'd 'changed the direction of surfing'. It was a pretty big call but I had no real beef with it. I know the boards were different then, but he was never staccato, there was nothing mechanical or predictable in how he surfed, and certainly none of that jumping up and down trying to carry through to the six inch re-form on the beach. If the wave was finished, or wasn't there in the first place, neither was he. His surfing flowed, if that's the phrase. He always came off as smoothly as he stroked in.

No sponsors had ever got hold of him either, in any shape or form. He was too much of a maverick for them. He never had any money and he only ever got out of Australia once. His type of outlook couldn't handle going foreign and all the bullshit associated with leaving home. The only time he went he was back inside a month, but even today after all this time they still talk about him over there.

No logos, no corny beach fashions ever hung off him, and you never saw him in those contrived magazine ads either. But it killed him just the same. It has a habit of doing that. The longer you think you've kept your options open the harder the gate finally snaps shut. We're all a bit fragile, I guess. And when the lights go out, if you can't see in the dark you've got problems.

I knew he'd battled alcohol; god knows I'd been with him enough in the early days to see what it was doing to him. After that it was heroin, and now it was cancer. Somehow he'd dragged himself down to the clifftop and sat there beside his wife, white-faced and pencil thin, just staring out. I don't know what thoughts were going through his mind. He was dead within six months. I found out later that on the morning he died he'd somehow crawled from his hospital bed to the window, and had collapsed from the effort of trying to raise the fixed window.

Jacky's talk finished fairly quickly. To be absolutely honest I don't think it had very much impact on most people. Sure, the snakes had impressed them for a time, but a steady diet of videos seemed to have laid waste whatever fertile ground there might have been. A notion like 'freedom', even with snakes, can't ever hope to compete with videos and the rest of the noise out there. Once Jacky finished, it was all downhill for us really.

The trouble came in the evening at the presentation. It was waiting for us when we arrived, thicker than the cocaine crystals on the toilet floor and just as slippery as the food plastered all over the dance floor. 'I think we should give this one a miss,' I'd said, but Jacky was adamant we should stick it out to the end. He had some notion that to bale out early was never the best way to go. After a day at the beach he wanted a drink, especially since the snakes had escaped in the backyard of my rented house and my neighbours had become agitated.

We began on a flagon of cheap port. Around us it was chaos. Somewhere in the lighted areas up front a presentation of sorts began. There were surfers wearing dinner suits making speeches thanking their sponsors and each other. Prizes and cheques were being thrown about like so much confetti, but at the back of the hall where we were, no one knew or cared what was going on.

A constant stream of food rained from one side of the hall to the other, glasses and bottles were spilt and broken at almost every table. Figures lay slumped on the floor, or against the walls, two of them with pools of vomit beside them. Between tables, and on the dance floor, over-amped figures gyrated this way and that, pushing and groping. Scuffles broke out here and there with angry strident voices. A woman was punched when she accidentally backed into someone at the edge of the dance floor.

In the midst of this mess I spotted trouble for us. He was wearing some sort of singlet because I remember his bare shoulders and the tattoos, and the way he'd stood back and sized us up. He must have thought about it for a while, because for a time nothing happened, and then he just sort of lunged at us out of the darkness.

'When I think of all the work that's been done to get surfing on its feet,' he was shouting at us, 'all the self-sacrifice for our sport, all the people who have given up absolutely everything to make it a mainstream sport, I could . . . I could . . .' He paused, momentarily lost for the right words. As his voice trailed off I thought we were out of it. But no such luck. 'And now this turns up,' he went on, his eyes glancing at Jacky, 'this fucking freedom crap.'

Before I realised how pissed he was I thought we were going to have real trouble. But just two steps back from us he launched his punch like someone heaving a shot put. It missed by a mile. His own momentum took him stumbling past Jacky, face first into the table edge and then to the floor. At least that's how I saw it.

There was another view, that Jacky's hands had moved. Nobody was sure of anything except that the guy's teeth were gone in a bubble of bloody foam and a muffled groan.

'Oh shit,' I heard someone say and after that I'm not sure of anything, because it all just erupted. We got out the side door before the police arrived, but we'd been worked over. It wasn't just us, there were others too. At one stage I'd warded off a broken bottle with my arm. A deep jagged cut was sliced into the flesh below the elbow, and it bled profusely, thick and deep red, down over my hand and fingers.

As we rested up in the darkness of the car park Jacky pressed his hands over the cut, holding it together. For a time I could see a stain oozing out between his stumpy, short-nailed fingers and feel a heat where they pressed against my arm. When he took his hand away, loose blood was still on my arm but the cut had gone. I wiped the blood away and all that remained was a thin pink line, like a surgical scar. The cut itself had gone. Just like that. It had gone.

Jacky never said a thing, not then, nor at any stage later.

I knew then that something had changed forever. The tide had been full and now it had turned. The mud flats of middle age can distance you from a lot of things, but that night I suddenly realised it was all finished for me. What was it someone had once written about 'the courage to lose sight of the shore'? How far offshore does a surfer ever go? 150 metres? 1500 metres?

I left Jacky at the station two days after all this. To this day I don't even know who won the contest. It's all the same after a while, and it's all been made to look the same.

Our faces were still puffy, red and blotched. Both my eyes were blackened, blue-yellow like the inside of hard-boiled eggs. Jacky's skin was sallow from the port. He hadn't stopped drinking since the snakes escaped. His hands were shaking.

That same morning he left we'd stood on a headland down from the rented house. The wind had laid down the coastal grasses and a moan had set up in the stunted trees. High above us, in the absolutely cloudless blue sky, six ibis had come down the coast, north to south. Things had been wet that autumn and lots of the nearby paddocks had low-lying water in them. Moments later another group of four appeared, then another. Soon they numbered perhaps fifteen or twenty birds.

At first the flight had no structure to it. It circled and wheeled, this way and that. But at last a central core of circling in one direction began to establish itself, and it was to this group that the others attached themselves. In this way the circle became bigger and bigger, the birds no longer black spots but now a mass, cohesive and purposeful. They then streamed out into a gigantic V that turned inland against the wind, and away from the sea.

I took this to mean the swell would drop out, which it did.

It was hinted to me later by my analyst that these things never really occurred. But I know they did. Some things are true even if they never happened. I know Jacky's now up north. When I last spoke to him he was running a prawn trawler somewhere up on the Queensland coast. He won't come down again in a hurry. He told me it's too cold south of Brisbane.

There's also the thin surgical-like scar on my left forearm. If all of this never happened, then how did that get there, and what healed it?

First published in *Caught Inside: Surf Writings and Photographs by Jack Finlay*, Stormy Weather Publications, 1992.

12

FULL MOON IN THE MENTAWAIS

Pro surfers, cameramen and a salty old surf pioneer go on a mission to promote surfing's humanitarian streak

Tim Baker

Airports ... I go to them seldom enough these days to have grown to love 'em again, by association. They are our portal to other worlds. Never mind the queues and customs and overpriced food and interminable waiting. You are going somewhere. And you are taking surfboards. How can that be bad?

The Mentawai Islands, off the west coast of Sumatra, are a modern surfing discovery and draw surfers from all over the world to feast on their array of perfect, remote surfing reefs.

There are at least five boatloads of surfers in the departure lounge for the Silk Air Flight to Padang, including an all-girls super crew of Lisa Andersen, Rochelle Ballard, Sofia Mulanovich, Chelsea Georgieson and Megan Abubo. Our blokes — Danny Wills, Dean Morrison, Jay 'Bottle' Thompson, Mitch Coleborn and Matt Wilkinson — assemble, predictably enough, around an airport bar for a few send-off Tiger Beers.

This swag of top professional surfers is travelling to the Mentawais to promote the work of Surf Aid, a humanitarian organisation supported by the worldwide surfing community to bring medical aid to the islands where malaria, cholera, malnutrition and other diseases are rife.

We're all here, except Lance Knight, and I pray the skipper from Yamba has made it this far. I needn't worry. He's already at the departure gate, amping to get out to the islands he helped discover.

The flight is delayed due to smoke haze. When we finally take off it is into a vast grey void in all directions, as far as the eye can see. What must Lance be thinking? He regales us with stories of that historic first trip. The mad bus ride from Medan. The local rock star he befriended. The light plane he hitched a ride on out to the islands with a local doctor. Then he was the only surfer, just about the only Westerner in Padang. Today he's part of a well-worn, lucrative tourism route he unwittingly helped forge.

Little islands appear out of the greyness, fringed by whitewater just off the Sumatran mainland, where there is usually no swell. Optimistic surf forecasts are bandied about wildly. The moon will soon be full — a portent for big waves according to Indonesian superstition. Then, suddenly, the mountains which ring Padang appear out the window, so close our wings look like they might brush the lush green foliage as we bank past and come in to land.

As we drive into Padang from the airport and the classic Indo chaos unfolds on the road in front of us, I turn around and see Lance and Matt Wilko on the seat behind me, side by side — the Indo veteran and the Indo virgin, thirty-seven years difference in age and a world of life experience apart, off together on an adventure, equally stoked and wide-eyed, taking it all in.

We get to Padang's only international hotel, the Bumi Minang, running late for a reception held by Surf Aid to explain their humanitarian work out in the islands. The Surf Aid crew are a fascinating mix of locals and expats from Australia, New Zealand and the United Kingdom, bound by a common vision of good health and empowerment for the long-suffering Mentawai people. Surf Aid founder Dr Dave Jenkins has some telling statistics: up to 50 per cent of kids will die by the age of five in the worst areas; 65 per cent of parents have lost at least one child. We watch shocking video footage of a man dying of cholera, positioned over a hole in the floor used as a toilet. His family, gathered helplessly around, are probably fated to succumb to the same disease, unaware that the milk of young coconuts — plentiful right outside their door — could keep them alive. It is this kind of knowledge that Surf Aid wants to spread.

There are some stirring case studies too — a little boy, stunted and sullen, brought back to good health after years of battling malaria, suddenly shooting up, luxurious hair growing long, running and playing, full of energy. The miracle treatment? A $10 mosquito net. For the first time in his young life, his system is not constantly battling the malaria parasites in his body.

A fierce storm is raging out at sea and everyone advises us against crossing the strait to the islands tonight. The pros quickly grab the last remaining rooms at the swank Bumi Minang, and the *Surfing World* team and Lance adjourn with the Surf Aid crew to a more humble but charming local hotel in a quaint converted old Dutch bank, the Batang Arau, named after the river it fronts. The downstairs bar is a kind of sanctuary for the Padang expat community and Surf Aid extended family. The *Surfing World* team fit right in, plied with vodka into the wee hours by a mad Englishman named Twisden. Twizz is one of the owners of our charter boat, the *Arimbi*, and an early financial backer of Surf Aid. He made his money in clubs and pubs in London in the '90s, then discovered surfing and pissed off with his girl for a year to go travelling and teach himself to surf in some of the world's most perfect waves. He is like a character from an Evelyn Waugh novel, *Brideshead Revisited* by the beach, and it's hilarious listening to surf talk spill out in his plum, proper English accent.

Lance is treated like a returning hero here. It seems like the first time anyone has made a fuss over the straight-shooting salty sea-dog from Yamba in his whole life. He is touched and a little embarrassed by the attention. 'These blokes are the real pioneers,' he reckons, giving credit to the several skippers gathered around our table. 'They're the ones who have made a go of it out here. I just stumbled on the place.'

By the end of the night, Lance has had several offers to skipper charter boats in the Mentawais, and an open ticket to jump aboard any of the boats free of charge whenever he returns with his two young boys. And it occurs to me, maybe these people wouldn't even be here now if it wasn't for Lance and his discovery. Surfers from all over the world have built lives here, married locals or met travellers and fallen in love; some have started families, businesses, built their homes here. Blokes like Albert, the skipper on *Indies Trader III*, who's married a local and started a coffee plantation and now supplies many hotels and charter boats in the area with the finest Sumatran coffee. This intermingling of cultures, this transplanting of lives on foreign soils, does more to bring us closer to our geographical neighbours in South East Asia than any foreign affairs policies and press statements emanating from Canberra. Alexander Downer, our Foreign Minister, ought to sit down with Lance or Albert over a few Bintangs at this noisy expats' pub in Padang to help him understand our place in the region.

We have an unscheduled day in Padang due to last night's storm. We cruise the bustling streets and are adopted by the inevitable local kids who want to act as guides and translators. We check out the local surf scene at the rivermouth of the

Batang Arau — the muddy brown river that winds through the town and deposits its filth into the ocean. The surf spot at the rivermouth is known as Cholera Creek, where dozens of Padang kids surf on battered old boards left behind by Western surfers. The waves look good — though a disturbing grey-brown in colour — a little peak with a long peeling left and shorter right. It's two to three feet and twenty or more kids are surfing it pretty well. The beach is covered in litter, including a couple of dead pigs and a cat. If they ever start a local chapter of the Surfrider Foundation here they'll have their work cut out for them.

Finally, it's time to board our boat, the *Arimbi*, which means 'goddess of good fortune'. We pile into minibuses and wind our way out of the teeming town, into the rural outskirts and on to the picturesque harbour — all lush mountainous jungle spilling to the sea, with ramshackle houses clinging to the coast and a gargantuan industrial port on the opposite side of the bay. Kids are riding a tiny little reefbreak on broken boards in the golden afternoon light. The waves are less than a foot and the kids get washed up on the beach over and over. It's as if our wake out in the islands is washing up here, spawning a whole new surf culture. They have uncanny natural balance. One kid is standing on the front half of a broken longboard, without fins, out the back of the break while he waits for waves, and gets washed in riding sideways.

This is the moment of truth for the surf charter passenger, when you first clap eyes on your floating home for the next ten days and discover whether it actually resembles the impressive photos on the travel agent's website. The *Arimbi* scrubs up all right and we clamber aboard, meet the crew, and claim bunks. The crew are classic, all-smiling, gracious, welcoming Indonesian family men in their thirties and forties or beyond — it's difficult to tell. They make us feel immediately at home on the *Arimbi*.

DAY 1: After motoring all night, we pull up at Telescopes just after dawn — a nicely tapered left-hand reef a few hundred metres off the inevitable palm-fringed island. It's two to three feet, a little morning sick but fun for a warm up.

Another boat pulls up in the afternoon and it gets kind of crowded. Even a canoeful of local kids arrive with boards and get among it, surfing with crude but effective styles and offering to sell us some skanky local weed. They appear to have a pretty nice lifestyle, living on a nearby island, with their own canoe, an outboard motor, fishing and surfing all day. They're young, in their late teens, early twenties maybe, and surfing must hold the promise of a new and exciting way of life.

DAY 2: The crew are up early to get us to Lance's Rights (the wave Lance discovered) at first light to greet the new swell. In our half-sleep we register only the whine of the anchor winch and the engine coughing to life, then the roll of the boat coaxes us back to sleep. One by one we drift up on deck as a grey, stormy morning dawns. You can just make out the jungle coast. There doesn't seem to be much sign of our swell but as Lance's Rights and the village of Katiet come into view there is mounting excitement. Black rain squalls are brewing up from the south. The wind is howling, raking the tops off the waves capping on the reef. Rain lashes down in sheets. I'm colder than I've ever been in Indo before. It's tough to gauge the surf conditions from the back but Deano, a veteran of eight visits to these islands, is convinced it's about six to eight feet. 'Look, look, it's doubling up,' he screams. He races to the top deck to get a board. He's brought no fewer than fourteen of them, in three boardbags, and leaves them strewn about the upper deck as he jumps off the side and strokes into the lineup. There's a helmeted bodyboarder from land already out. As we draw alongside we can see that Deano's right. Heaving walls unload on the reef, straining against the offshore and folding over into gaping caverns.

I watch Lance watching the surf and wonder what's going through his mind — but only for a moment. Aleks, our deckhand, has got the dinghy fired up and I jump in with a brand new seven-foot channel bottom for a ride out. Deano waves us away from the lineup, frothing like a maniac, not wanting any wake to distort the contoured faces of the rifling tubes, and quickly strokes into three long barrels in succession, with his perfect, compact style. Lance is next out, with his helmet and trusty yellow semi-gun. There are some solid, intimidating sets, but Deano has it instantly wired. Lance gets pitched on his first wave and several others, but is charging, keen to get thoroughly reacquainted. He has a couple of trips in over the reef and loses some skin. Welcome back.

Within twenty minutes a second boat, *Huey*, has pulled up, looking like something out of 'McHales Navy', an ex-patrol boat with the full Hawaiian North Shore contingent onboard. The Wolf Pak, the Pipe Posse, whatever you want to call them — Kala Alexander, Myles Padaca, Brian Pacheco and all the boyz — one of the most intimidating packs of surfers you could possibly run into out here. Lance is a bit surprised by the instant crowd. 'Hey, there are a few too many out here. Someone might have to go in,' he quips good-naturedly, unaware who he's talking to. One of the larger Hawaiians chortles, 'Change of shift, brah.' It feels like things could get tense, but the moment passes. Everyone shares happily enough. A sociologist would have a field day, as our two tribes settle into the lineup, make connections, establish a pecking order.

I see more outrageous barrels in two hours than I've seen for a surf-starved month at home. It's Willsy's first time here and he is blown out. 'One of the best right-handers in the world,' he reckons. Deano stays out for five hours, getting countless barrels. Gradually word spreads among the Hawaiians that Lance is *the* Lance — pioneer of this place, after whom the wave is named — and he's given a bit of space in the lineup. Kala even calls him into a couple. But it's a rugged welcome back just the same. I eventually retreat to the boat and watch.

Lance and I go into the beach to look for Hosen and his family, who looked after Lance all those years ago — took him in, fed him for two weeks, all with little common language and refusing all Lance's offers of money. We don't even know if the man's still alive. Lance talks to a teenage boy on the beach and gets directions to Hosen's place and before we know it, there he is, coming out of his house.

'Hosen, it's Lance,' Lance announces warmly. Hosen lets out a loud cheer of recognition. They both seem a bit stunned, standing face to face, the realisation sinking in. Hosen is in his sixties but looks fit as a fiddle, tall, proud, erect, not stooped at all.

I want to capture the moment and I watch it all on my little video viewfinder, mesmerised. They shake hands, exchange a few words of Indonesian. 'Lance, Lance,' Lance confirms, poking himself in the chest. Hosen looks about as if for witnesses to this wonder, puts an arm round the Australian and rubs his back warmly. Lance has tears in his eyes.

Hosen's wife comes out. 'Lance!' Hosen tells her.

'Aaaaahhh,' she sighs in surprise.

There is much animated conversation, they invite us inside and give us cans of Coke and cups of tea and crackers. They look to be prospering. Hosen has a solid timber and concrete two-storey house, stores of food and drinks piled up in one room, guest accommodation upstairs, where four South American surfers are currently staying. Lance unpacks his bag of gifts, tools, medicine, clothes for the kids and toys; and there is much exchanging of news in Lance's broken Indo and their few words of English. Hosen takes us out the back to show off his new generator that provides the house with electricity. Surfing has clearly been good to them. They still remember the exact date Lance arrived in their village — 18 March 1991, the day surfing began in Katiet, and the catalyst for their new prosperity.

We go down to the beach to take some photos of the happy reunion, and there's the wave, the source of their new wealth, still barrelling and spitting away. We say our farewells for the time being and head back to the boat.

The arvo session is gold, literally, the sun breaking through the clouds for the first time all day and bathing the pulsing lineup in the most heavenly golden light shining straight into the eye of the barrel. The photographers are euphoric. Everyone is stoked. The girls' boat pulls up and several of them have a serious dig amid the testosterone-packed lineup. The sets are starting to do that double-up thing, capping on an outside reef then spilling and spewing and reforming on the inside reef into caves of outrageous proportions. Wilko and I watch Deano drive into one from so far back that we just stare at each other in disbelief as he pops out the end.

It's an amped boat that night. Day two and we're all buzzing. Lance can't contain his excitement. 'One of the most special days of my life,' he tells me. 'To speak Indo, "pagi khasus". To return after thirteen, fourteen years, the emotion of meeting Hosen and his wife and his family, going in there and finding out that he's still alive and still happy and healthy — it's amazing ... When I first came, the kids were all little dirty urchins in rags. That's why I brought all those clothes for them. Today when I went in there, there's kids riding brand new pushbikes on their little road in there. The young guys are all well dressed, they've got name-brand boardies on. This village has become prosperous because of surfing, so my coming here — I've done something good for them. Surf Aid has been started and that's saved thousands of lives in these islands. I'm awed by it.'

Another unbelievable dinner of steak and mash and vegies, and calamari. Couple of cold Bintangs, much excited surf babble about the day, a few quiet reflective moments pissing and fishing off the side, star gazing, or up top chilling in what has become the hip hop lounge. And then bed. Sleep comes easily.

DAY 3: The next day dawns grey, rainy and windy. Andy, Bottle and I go for a paddle but it's sideshore/onshore, a bit smaller, still some sets but bumpy and hard to surf. I'm turning out the back of a little close-out when I feel a sharp shot of hot pain up the inside of my left knee. I've never had knee problems but everyone reckons it sounds like a strain or small tear in the medial ligament. Rest, ice, compression and elevation is Willsy's prescription. It's a cruel blow — being on a surf charter boat out here, with waves, and unable to surf.

We head to Macaronis for the afternoon session, a couple of hours motoring south. It's small, grey, overcast, a bit bumpy but the groms are all over it. It's the perfect contrast to yesterday's dramatic surf — fun, playful, the ideal skatepark for the young blokes and their antics.

DAY 4: Fun waves at Macaronis, everyone going mad. I still can't surf, and I devote myself to mastering the iMovie program on my laptop.

DAY 5: We check a little, out-of-the-way right and Deano jumps straight into it — apparently small, overcast, inconsistent. Willsy goes over for a look, barely interested, reckons there's one wave every ten minutes, enough for one person only, but jumps in anyway. The others go over to Thunders which is bigger but more exposed to the wind. I take little interest, in my cocooned edit suite downstairs. When Easty stumbles in a couple of hours later, eyes bulging, tongue flapping, barely able to get the words out about the life-altering session he's just witnessed, I figure he's joking. But he's not. As soon as they got out there, the wind dropped, the sets pumped, and Willsy and Deano enjoyed their own private barrelfest, with Easty and Hilton on hand to shoot the steely, sheet-glass drain pipes. 'That was the session of the trip,' Easty babbles, a big call after Lance's Rights.

The others are similarly gobsmacked. 'It wasn't big, but like the most perfect Kirra you could ever get on a reef, like a bullshit section of Kirra,' Willsy says. 'In the end we were letting eight second barrels go, waiting for bigger ones. Crazy, mate, absolutely crazy.'

Finally, satisfied that I have truly missed a life-changing session, I return to the edit suite to lick my wounds. The trip, it seems, is now officially a corker. Anything beyond this is a bonus.

DAYS 6 TO 8: The mid-section of our trip is characterised by unfavourable winds, bone-jarring journeys from one end of the islands to the other into howling headwinds, and the obligatory big night on the Bintangs and duty-free. Still, the Mentawai Islands have been good to us, and our moral duty out here is to rendezvous with the Surf Aid crew and promote their tireless work.

DAY 9: We've had all kinds of waves in all kinds of conditions. I've ventured back out with a heavily strapped knee and done some straight line trimming. The crew seemed relieved to have me off the boat, instead of skulking around scribbling in my notepad.

We have one final surf at Burgerworld and run into the all-star girls' team and a crew of gung-ho Frenchmen. It's a long way to come to surf with twenty people. We leave them to it and go off to our Surf Aid appointment.

The weather's looking ominous and the crew are freaking about heading in to Padang as early as possible. It's pissing with rain and looks like our planned village visit could be a bit of a write-off. But good old Lance stands firm, insisting we've come this far and can't go home without doing our bit for Surf Aid. His impassioned speech rallies the troops and we brave the rain to see first-hand the miraculous work of the Surf Aid team. Taileleu is a picturesque village, surrounded by dense jungle and mountains perpetually capped with rainclouds. It has the highest rainfall in the entire islands. We rendezvous with the team aboard *Indies Trader II*, whose skipper Martin Daly has graciously volunteered to bring the doctors out here. We head into the village with Willsy and Deano for a bit of a photo op to promote the cause. Kids clamour wherever we go. We wander the village with Dr Dave and entourage, meet some of the kids Surf Aid has helped save, talk to mothers whose kids are now thriving, sleeping safely under Surf Aid mosquito nets.

Easty is shooting some photos of Dr Dave, the surfers and a gaggle of village kids when a local shaman comes strolling along the track, with exquisite timing. For 20 000 rupiah (about three bucks), he agrees to pose for some shots — clove ciggy dangling from his lips, assorted leaves and feathers decorating his arms and legs, a yellow colouring smeared over his face.

It's easy to see this place as an unspoilt paradise, with its quaint thatched roof cottages, vegetable gardens, fruit trees, happy kids playing in puddles. Yet life here requires an extreme fatalism, a preparedness to watch children, loved ones, even yourself waste away and die from the local array of tropical diseases, with little chance of defending anyone. As a parent, I can't begin to imagine the anguish. Dave and his team have been out here for four years now. The locals didn't know what to make of them at first — thought they were missionaries, feral surfers, maybe refugees from the modern world — until slowly they realised the team were simply here to help. 'A hand up, not a hand out' is Dave's guiding philosophy and his greatest goal is to make himself redundant here, to educate and empower the communities to claim their right to good health. It's inspiring stuff, and has transformed surfers' presence here from just one more wave of exploiters to humane and caring partner in a better future for the Mentawais.

If the popularity of the surf here can result in improved health and prosperity for the people, and provide an economy not dependent on logging the trees or dynamiting the reefs, then the influx of surfers seems a small price to pay.

The rest of our crew are watching *Jackass* on the video when we return from the village, and the contrast couldn't be more dramatic. Wealthy, white, First World guys deliberately injuring themselves for public amusement, when they have the benefits of health care and modern hospitals, versus a Third World village fighting for survival in a remote, harsh environment. I wonder how long we can deny these people the blessing of such sophisticated Western culture!

A boat trip to the Mentawais is nothing new, but it is now part of our surfing landscape and we must surely seek to understand rather than simply search and destroy. There is a sad irony, I reflect, in us wealthy Westerners cruising the Indonesian archipelago in luxury boats, while desperate refugees set out from Indonesia, crammed into unseaworthy vessels. And we barely blink when they sink and drown by the hundreds or are locked up like criminals, while we surf and feast and play in the same ocean. When Lance wandered into Katiet nearly fifteen years ago, unexpected and uninvited, he was welcomed with open arms, fed and housed and treated like an honoured guest — not persecuted as the first wave of an imminent invasion. It's a

PETER EASTWAY

James 'Bottle' Thompson enjoying the remote Mentawai surf adventure that draws surfers from around the world.

PETER EASTWAY

Dean Morrison tackles a big, perfect wave at Lance's Rights in the Mentawai Islands.

Australia's queen of the waves Pam Burridge, carving cleanly at Hawaii's Rocky Point and blazing a trail for women surfers everywhere.

Pam claims the Billabong Pro at Sunset Beach, Hawaii, in 1989, far-fetched teenage dreams finally realised.

Lisa Anderson setting new standards for women's surfing at the Billabong Pro contest in France in 2000.

Nat Young in a reflective mood, at a golden late afternoon session.

The moment of truth for one hapless surfer, as a takeoff goes badly wrong at Hawaii's Pipeline.

Ian Walsh tackles the huge waves of the appropriately named Jaws, an outer reef off the coast of Maui, Hawaii. These waves are so big and travel so fast, the surfer has to be towed in by jet ski.

JOLI

Derek Ho turns around a mountain of whitewater at Hawaii's famed Sunset Beach.

TONY HARRINGTON/HARROART.COM

DAVE SPARKES

ABOVE: Andy King at home in the kind of big hollow waves he thrives in. RIGHT: Andy struggles to come to terms with his ear implant.

NATHAN SMITH

NATHAN SMITH

Andy regaining his surfing confidence after losing his hearing in a street fight.

Kelly Slater displays his command and confidence at the Pipeline Masters, Hawaii, but he can still be found there long after the cameras and contests have packed up and gone home.

Troy Brooks gets his moment centre stage during the photo-feeding frenzy that is the North Shore of Oahu, Hawaii, each December.

TED GRAMBEAU

Tom Carroll gets in some tube time to unwind after the rigours of Hawaiian inter-island paddle racing.

TED GRAMBEAU

The kind of powerful remote Western Australian desert-coast reef wave that draws a hardy breed of surfers looking to lose themselves in the ocean.

blessed life we surfers lead, managing to pursue our bliss in a tortured world. The bridges we build out there are a measure of our humanity and, in some small way, might help make the world a better, safer place for us all.

First published in *Surfing World* magazine, 2004.

For more information on Surf Aid go to: www.surfaidinternational.org

13

WHAT WOMEN WANT

Back in 1992, a world champion accurately forecast the present boom in women's surfing

Pam Burridge

Slowly, ceremoniously, the parade edged through the small American town. Groups of two or three girls perched on car roofs and bonnets waved to the assembled townsfolk. One of the cars drew more reverence. The words emblazoned on the doors 'Margo Oberg World Surfing Champion' cried out for more respect.

The sun beat down in the hot New York summer. The cheering and flag waving continued until all the cars had passed and the people of Hampton Bays returned to their daily business.

I was impressed — embarrassed but impressed. At fifteen years of age, I had just placed second to Margo Oberg in the Hampton Bays Women's Classic, upsetting Lynne Boyer in a split decision on the way.

The fresh wad of prize money, the special treatment and infantile hangover all added to the altered version of reality this fifteen-year-old saw. The road to fame and fortune beckoned as a mermaid lures sailors to treacherous rocks. I was sold on the idea of professional surfing, but little did I know the testing times to come.

I started surfing with the attitude that I was going to do it no matter what, regardless of what others would think or say. My parents were actually very encouraging once they recognised my enthusiasm. This is not the case for many girls. Acceptance from their peers and the hierarchy at the beach prevents them from venturing into the ocean clutching a potentially embarrassing surfboard. If, in fact, one gets past the first few sessions then the sheer difficulty of grasping the basic techniques can become discouraging. Too many nosedives and heckling from twelve-year-old aggro grommets sees adolescent girls scrambling for the safety of the beach where they, sadly, remain.

Some come through these challenges, hanging on to the feeling captured on that first successful ride, to follow a lifestyle centred around the rewards of the ocean and the surf. These characters, in the past, have by necessity been a hardy lot — perpetuating the image of the butch, unfeminine surfie chick.

Not so nowadays. Most of the obstacles (other than nosediving) can be overcome by knowledge, encouragement and experience gained in surf schools and clinics. Girls particularly can benefit from the embarrassment-free environment experienced at such clinics. These new surf converts can now look ahead to where surfing can take them. People have been there before and beaten the path, if not paved it.

Changes for professional women's surfing have been gradual but significant. There were eighteen events scheduled in 1992 compared with five in 1981 when I first joined the tour. Prize money has remained low to help the circuit grow but, ironically, it's the crippling costs of getting to all these locations and events that may prohibit many young hopefuls from joining the tour.

Fortunately for the health of women's pro surfing, the lure of the number one spot is still just as strong as it was for me at the age of twelve. It's not the money the girls are after, it's the lifestyle and the fame, the thrill of competition and the self-satisfaction of attaining goals. The question of money comes later, long after the desire has been lit in the heart, burning irrationally, forcing career decisions that leave Ma and Pa scratching their concerned heads.

I've seen girls on tour who refuse to keep account of their expenses because the ridiculous debt begs unanswered questions: 'Why do I do this? It costs me a fortune and I'm miserable from losing most of the time.'

Perhaps the myth of the perfect wave has transformed into the myth of the perfect heat or perfect performance in the mind of the young competitor and it draws them on, promising a better next result, better next year . . . better grow up or die from disillusionment. And through all this we keep coming back for more, churning out champions and contest casualties by the truckload.

In the '80s, the style and grace era of Hawaiian dominance was challenged and defeated. The pro tour went to the beachbreaks around the world and the champions of the future had to adapt. The domination that four-time world champion Frieda Zamba enjoyed during the '80s suggests she adapted best. Her athleticism and focus oozed professionalism, her 360s and aerials broke new ground. Turning points for women's surfing have come courtesy of individuals making their statement. Seeing a seventeen-year-old Wendy Botha streaking along a clean Burleigh Heads wall on a magic twin fin that obeyed her every command was one such landmark. The skinny blonde South African came to Australia for the first time in 1985, at the invitation of Stubbies contest director Bill Bolman. Bill, the used car salesman, had seen Wendy at home and urged her to venture out and kick some arse. Bill created a women's event as an adjunct to the men's Stubbies almost purely to showcase Wendy's talents. Luckily for our collective Australian ego, I managed to edge her out in the final of the four-woman Stubbies. But after a frustrated career start, Wendy went on to collect three world titles of her own.

In the wake of Frieda and Wendy's successes came today's most-talked-about female surfers. The professional pioneering had largely been done and some new faces were ready to cut loose.

The time-honoured testing ground for aspiring pros has to be Bells each Easter. A ridiculously small fifteen-year-old Pauline Menczer first made her pilgrimage south under the raucous guidance of (a since mellowed) Kathy Anderson and came within an interference call of defeating Frieda Zamba in round one.

Pauline's world-title ambitions may be thwarted by any number of girls, the most noticeable being Lisa Andersen. Much has been written about Lisa's free surfing but a vision remains with me from Lisa's final competitive heats as a trialist. It was a small day at Sunset Point where the Underwets Pro was underway, methodically expelling the unlucky or unworthy. I bobbed up and down in the calm sea chatting to other caddies and photographers. Interrupted by a set of four-footers, our attention turned to a well positioned paddler. The young Floridian, still relatively unknown at this time, came hurtling towards the floating gallery and unleased the most INSANE power slide cutback — reminiscent of Luke Egan's trademark move.

'WHOA ... who's that girl?!' a babbling photographer Warren Bolster exclaimed, barely retaining his balance atop his surfmat, still rocking from Lisa's foamy trail.

'That's Lisa Andersen, she does that all the time.' I gulped, wondering how the surfer I was caddying for would ever get out of this heat and indeed how any of us would win anything against that new attack of surfing.

Andersen's impact on women's surfing has been great. Firstly, it has reinforced the need to raise performance levels. Secondly, she has forged new ground in the way her value is not directly linked with contest results and world ratings. Her surfing does the promoting and she works the cameras well. The surfing magazines have been quick to publish shots of her with headlines, 'The Best Woman Surfer in the World'. Her sponsors are surf industry through and through and her involvement with them, and the magazine response, may help to erode the company line: 'Women's surfing doesn't sell product.'

With more girls surfing and the sport becoming more accessible through schools and clinics, the company line may have to change to suit the changing times. The window through which Lisa has climbed on sheer ability and good looks may blow a breeze of fresh attitudes over the careers of the next generation of female hotties.

Already teams are springing up, clued into this new trend — women's products being promoted by female surfers. A healthy rivalry stirring between swimwear heavies translates into promotion and sponsorship of their team members and augurs well for the future of women's surfing.

No more do we need argue whether women surf as well as men. What matters is that they are surfing better all the time. If the history of surfing tells us anything, youth will find new expression for their obsession. The phenomenal improvement we have seen in men's pro surfing in recent years tells me that women's surfing can make the same improvements.

Through no fault of our own, I believe we've given the guys about a decade headstart. So let's leave the judgements for the future, and surf for today.

First published in *Surfing Life* magainze, 1992.

14

EVEREST RISING

The 100-foot wave? Does it exist? Is it rideable? And if so, who the hell is likely to try?

Matt Griggs

On 8 February 2001, a 12-metre disc in the Bering Straight recorded a wave measuring 14.45 metres, before becoming capsized by its subject.

But this 55 feet of liquid Everest, probably headed to Alaska, gave rise to the suggestion: what if a swell like this reached a perfect reef? How big can the ocean get? Can surfers ride it? Are we getting out of our realm?

In February 2004, Jaws got one of the biggest swells in recorded history. Out in the north Pacific, buoy 51001 recorded the largest single wave height peaking at 7.56 metres (20 to 25 feet). Because most of a swell travels below water, when it hits a shallow reef it abruptly grows in size. This therefore translated to 60-foot faces at Jaws. Massive right? Well, apparently, that's just the lemon next to a potentially preposterous pie. If a swell as big as the one recorded in the Bering Straight in 2001 reached Jaws, its height would produce 165-foot faces. If a swell like this peaked at an open ocean reef shaped as perfectly as Cortes Bank, you could multiply the swell height by a factor of 3.5 to four. That's 220 foot!

Think big wave surfing can't go any further? We're only at the bottom of a massive, moving mountain — and for the first time, technology is catering for a sport that goes way beyond extreme.

The swell that drowned the buoy in 2001 was not the largest recorded wave, nor will it be the last. According to Bill Sharp, Project Director of the Billabong Odyssey (an open-ended big budget big wave hunting mission), 'Since the era of big wave surfing began in '97, 30-foot waves were the biggest. Now we're riding 60-foot faces. The weather goes in cycles and I think we can see 30 to 50 per cent bigger waves, no problem. Everest is never going to get higher — but there is always a bigger storm.'

One such storm occurred on 19 November 1991, when a six-metre, boat-shaped NOMAD hull recorded the all-time highest significant wave height (16.91 metres). If this swell had reached Cortes, it would make Mike Parsons' famous wave there (an

80-foot face) look like a pimple on the Pacific's arse. It would have been around 240 feet! Just stop and think about that for a while . . .

'And remember,' says Bill, 'that reading was just the biggest only since buoys have become pretty reliable and numerous in the last twenty years or so. How big it has been prior to that we don't know. How big it will get over the next hundred years is anyone's guess.'

True, the buoys in the north Pacific have only been in place since the '70s. But, as the readings have only been accurate in the last two decades, we're still only learning. To complicate matters, the weather travels in cycles. Introduce *el nino* conditions, where you're getting more warm water (energy) in areas of the ocean where it will interact with cold air (activity) and you get a concoction to produce some pretty violent storms. But more importantly, these big storms might track closer to potential reefs, or outer-ocean bommies (bomboras) and islands. It seems the discovery of Cortes Bank has been more a prelude than a revelation. 'Somewhere out there might well be a reef that does even better,' says Bill. Shane Dorian, who is now full-time on the Billabong Odyssey to hunt massive waves agrees. 'I think we will ride waves in the next five years that are twice the size of any waves ever ridden.'

Waves are created by wind. But it's not just a stronger wind that creates bigger waves. The longer the wind has been blowing strong, the bigger and more powerful the swell it creates.

According to Bill, there's an optimal distance from the storm at which the swell is the biggest. 'Somewhere between 1000 to 1500 miles away from the centre of the storm is where the waves are converted into the largest possible swell height. Ten years ago, we didn't have a clue about that. Now we're finding waves that fit that category.'

Bill, and others, spend their time scouring nautical maps, checking reef configurations, depths of potential bommies in the middle of the ocean, buoy reports and weather charts. If there's a swell, they know about it. The elusive 100-foot wave target is starting to look more like a first step than an unrealistic goal. Having said that, the Odyssey is offering a million dollar bounty to the first surfer to ride a 100-foot wave.

When you familiarise yourself with the way the lows track, it seems that west-facing coastlines at certain latitudes fit the profile for discovery. 'The northwest face of the Hawaiian island chain is one example,' says Bill. 'There's about 1500 kilometres of coastline waiting to be explored properly. We're just familiar with the first islands. There are also atolls all over the south Pacific. And Chile — I reckon that is the end of the rainbow. It has all the key elements. The Atlantic also holds plenty of potential — the Canaries, the Azores and the west coast of Africa. And of course Australia — there are places in Oz we're just discovering that could be insane.'

'As you know we are pretty protective of our little wave,' says Jake Paterson, of a new discovery in the southwest. He recently scored it around 30 feet. 'The last time we surfed there the swell was huge. But it has to be really, really clean to surf it. I guess it would handle about 30 to 40 feet. I think we can get bigger swell, easy! But never clean. In winter our storms are out of control and the ocean gets fucken' huge, but you would never be able to ride it because of the winds and stuff.'

It's ironic that the very thing that creates the swell — wind — also has the power to destroy it. Shane Dorian is starting to realise this. He has been to most of these waves and has also been in the process of mapping potential discoveries, but his mind is pretty made up on where the biggest waves will occur. 'Definitely Cortes Bank,' he says. 'Just because of its location.'

But that's just waves that we already know about. No one knows about the other potential spots. 'Tahiti gets way bigger swell than what you've seen at Teahupo'o,' says Tahitian surfer Verea 'Poto' David. 'There are some days that are so big, I don't go anywhere near it. We have other places we are now finding that get even bigger.'

All you have to do is pick up a map of the world and you can see the potential places. Because no one's standing there watching, waves are going unnoticed, unridden. Right now, there's probably a 50-foot swell waiting to quadruple in size on a reef we've never known about. We used to turn our back on these swells. Now, there are not only people finding them, there are people willing to ride them.

One of the gnarliest moments in recent big wave history, was recalled by Ken 'Skindog' Collins as he witnessed the near death experience of Darryl 'Flea' Virostko while surfing at Mavericks:

Back in 1997 or so during that *el nino* year on a huge 25-foot plus northwest swell (before tow) I watched Flea paddle for a wave and miss it. What happened next made me sick and still does to this day. The next wave was a 25-foot double hell beast that just backed off forever and then fully unleashed, throwing 50 feet out. I barely made it over the top and looked back to see how my buddy was doing. He was getting off his board and diving. I thought he was good, 'cause the lip was throwing over him. Well I was wrong; he should have taken his leash off, 'cause it turned into the rope of death. He almost made it through the other side, but as his hand came through the 25-foot back, he stopped and got dragged back over the falls into pure horror. It looked as if the devil himself had grabbed the Flea and dragged him down to hell. Except hell would be a vacation compared to a Mavz [Maverick's] beating. I looked in, scanning ground zero for pieces of board and body parts.

He ended up popping up about 200 metres inside on half of his board. He looked dead but paddled his half gun towards the shoulder. But the party was not over yet; the devil saved the best dance for last. As he scrambled for the shoulder like a wounded animal, another set loomed in on him. The set roared over him pushing him into the rocks. If you've never seen the rocks at Mavz believe me, they are fucked. Seven or so, ranging in 10- to 15-foot tall and 20- to 30-foot long all jagged and full of barnacles and looking like a mouth full of teeth. One even looks like a giant shark fin, I swear to God.

Our superhero wasn't looking too good, and if there were a rescue ski around this wouldn't have happened. My chick was on the cliff filming the whole thing. As he went into the Death rocks, he should've taken off his leash again. He went through the rocks pretty nicely and looked like he was safe. But all of a sudden he stopped and got pulled under water. His leash had become snagged and also the tail of his board! Anchored into the rocks. So there he was, standing in three- to four-feet of water, right in front of hundreds of people, drowning, and nobody could help him. My chick was filming and screaming at the same time. (Epic footage.) You could hear the crowd screaming and yelling, 'Somebody do something!' But nobody could. Our hero was pinned to the bottom with every wave and couldn't move. As soon as it would back off for a second, he'd try to take his leash off and then get hit by the next wave and pinned down again. This happened for like five waves in a row, and he looked like a wet rag doll just getting weaker and weaker. Out the back was an endless set and our little buddy looked doomed, DOOMED I tell ya! But all of a sudden by the grace of God, Flea's leash snapped and let him free. He floated into the beach as if he saw death. He walked away talking to nobody, leaving everyone in silence . . .

Later that night he told us that he thought he was dead and got a little scared. But not that scared, 'cause the little bastard is up there every swell over 20 foot, has won all three of the Mavz Events, and has taken the throne as King of Mavericks. Hail to the Flea!!!!

Remember growing up as grommets? Waves like this weren't a part of your reality. There were always days when it was too big to surf and finding somewhere clean would be the issue at hand. Even in Hawaii, the options closed out when Waimea Bay did.

That's not the case anymore. The question now is where is it bigger? The guys asking the question are the same guys surfing it: Mike Parsons, Brad Gerlach, Laird Hamilton, Shane Dorian, Carlos Burle, Ross Clarke-Jones, Tony Ray, Cheyne Horan, Darrick Doerner, Garret MacNamara. But there are also some low-key, underground chargers. Guys like Rusty Long, who basically spends his unfunded time travelling the world looking for massive waves. He was also one of the four surfers out at Cortes Bank last time it got ridiculous. His summary of big wave surfing is not only inspiring, but also is pure and uncorrupted by an industry more after a big buck than a big wave.

'Well, for me, surfing big waves has been a natural progression over the years that has now become normality,' says Rusty. 'If there's a big swell brewing, we're on it. It's really as simple as that. Chasing the feeling and trying to get one that exceeds the others — and to achieve that, you have to continually test yourself mentally and physically in situations of consequence and I figure that's enhancing our raw survival instincts also. I get off on that — the continual challenge makes me happy. That true, *true* feeling of being alive that you get from being among such massive forces of energy, especially after taking a hectic wipeout. A good beating time and again is essential.'

Rusty speaks of the subject with a licence no one can question, borne from the weird creativity that draws him to the waves that can kill him. As far as big wave surfing goes, it's more ticker than talent — and like most things the skill comes from experience only. 'I was out at Jaws on that big day,' says Tony Ray about one of the largest swells in recent years. We are at Bells Beach where he is driving the jet ski for the surfers in the Rip Curl Pro. It's a far cry from Jaws, but it pays the bills that allow him to follow his abnormally sized heart. 'The lefts were actually cleaner,' he continued. 'The wind was offshore and there were these three foot bumps coming back at us, as big as that,' he says, pointing to a chair. 'You're going so fast and you've got no hope of getting a rail through that — you've just got to pick long, safer lines.' At the moment, experience is the basis for big wave surfing. That's why Laird Hamilton and Tony Ray and guys like Cheyne Horan are the best. 'Laird is by far and away the best big wave surfer,' says Shane Dorian. 'At least 50 per cent better than anyone else.' But despite this experience there must come a point when they are out of their depth.

*   *   *

At what point are we likely to get killed? It's a question that everyone thinks about, but never brings up. So far, generally, everyone who's drowned while big wave surfing has either been knocked out, by their board or the bottom, or trapped in a cave. And some of these were quite recently: Donnie Solomon, Mark Foo and Todd Chesser all lost their lives while chasing their ultimate thrill.

'The worst I ever experienced was at Mavericks,' says Mike Parsons. 'It's the eeriest wave I've ever surfed. It has that vibe, when you go out there — you feel vulnerable. I went down on a huge set. When I was under water I felt someone brush past me. I had no idea at the time, but it was Mark Foo, just before he drowned.'

These guys can hold their breath for a very long time if they have to. 'It's amazing how the human body fights death,' says Kieren Perrow, who's had his share of two-wave hold-downs. If you really have to, even after the exertion of paddling and surfing, you can hold your breath for a while. At least, longer than you think. But within a couple of minutes, your brain will trigger an involuntary muscle contraction to breathe. And if you are still down, you will be breathing water; the only hope that then remains is resuscitation. That speaks of just how important your partner is when you're surfing big waves. They're your lifeline, way after you let go of the rope and enter the wave's dictation.

Here's the scenario — surfers being towed by jet ski are going around 50 kph. That's very fast to come to a sudden stop — hard enough to knock you out. But with life jackets on, big wave surfers are putting the trust in their partners. If they do get knocked out, their partners are nearby on the jet skis, waiting to get them out of danger, or if they have to, resuscitate them.

Poto has warned surfers that Teahupo'o is too dangerous once it gets to a certain size and Shane Dorian, who even looks forward to riding 100-foot Cortes, agrees. 'I think people are getting out of their depth at Teahupo'o for sure.'

Out in the middle of the ocean, or at most big wave spots, the bottom is not always the problem, as these areas are generally pretty deep. There are other factors to worry about. Ross Clarke-Jones and Tony Ray were mowed down on their ski a few years back at huge Outer Log Cabins in Hawaii. Is there a size where a surfer simply cannot outrun a huge wave (remember, the bigger the wave, the faster it moves) and instead becomes engulfed by it like an avalanche? Is there a limit?

'I don't think so,' says Bill Sharp. 'If you found an oily, glassy, perfect wave, a surfer can ride it. The big thing is the gravity of the lip following. If you can stay ahead of the lip, that's the only scientific limit. You won't be pulling in, but you can ride it.' The big 'X' factor is the bump. Like Tony Ray said, 'It's hard riding a 60-foot face with bumps the size of chairs coming at you.'

The refinement of tow-in surfboards has escaped the grasp of the average surfer. The boards the big wave surfers are riding are half the length — from six-foot to six-foot-six maybe to ride a 70-foot face. They are smaller, narrower and heavier. They'll help you stick to the face of a massive swell, but the bump cannot be conquered by equipment.

'Unless you have Laird thighs,' says Bill, 'you won't handle the bounce, but on glassy waves, anything is possible.'

But while all these phenomenal advancements are being made, it's not the leading surfers who are getting out of their depth. Before jet skis were introduced to bridge the gap paddling couldn't, you used to have to ride giant Waimea and do your time, before you progressed to waterman status. Guys like Laird Hamilton, Cheyne Horan, Darrick Doerner, Ross Clarke-Jones ... they've caught as many of these waves as we have shories and have made the natural progression. But there are some new cowboys putting themselves in life-threatening situations.

'Now, this year, people are trying to enter the XXL Big Wave Awards who can barely make it to their feet,' says Bill. 'We kind of went through a period where everyone knew their safety techniques and their team. They'd all come from paddling in at Big Bay and Mavericks and Jaws and so on, so they have made a natural progression. We had some deaths during that learning curve and I think we are going back to that era, where we might see more. All of a sudden, people think if you're a bungy-jumper, or an extreme skier, that you can buy a jet ski and take on Jaws. So that's what worries me more than anything.'

In terms of other technological developments we are becoming more aware of our limitations. As far as safety goes, I guess the first question is the obvious one that we often avoid — why do you die? And if it is because we run out of oxygen, would a little tank of oxygen strapped to your life vest be a safety innovation?

'Sometimes the solution creates other problems,' says Bill. 'If you take a full breath while you're down there, then come up, you'll die. Anyone who has dived knows that your lungs expand when you ascend [as water pressure decreases your lungs expand like a balloon, so divers are taught to slowly let air out as they approach the surface so their lungs don't burst].'

Life vests or jackets are of paramount importance in this scenario. The beating may knock out the surfer, but as long as he gets to the top, help is at hand. Nobody wanted to wear lifejackets at first, thinking you need to be able to penetrate the water. Now, they're thinking that floating is a good thing — it's better to get smashed and washed through the inside impact zone than not come up at all.

'I think there will be a lot of refinement in surfboard design, especially fins,' says Dorian. At present, surfboard design is struggling to keep up with the new pressures surfers are finding under their feet. Right now, some Hawaiians are experimenting with boards in the five-foot mark. The simple philosophy is more board is harder to control. So in a way, it's like we are back in the era of the shortboard revolution.

So will we surf a 100-foot wave? 'Yes,' says Shane Dorian. Without inspiring religious analogies, it's hard to imagine something you haven't seen. But science has a habit of applying reason to things unknown — and humans, through their discomfort of all things unknown, have a habit of conquering them with science. 'People at first just scoffed at it,' says Bill of the 100-foot mark set by the Odyssey. 'It was only a few months later we had an 85- to 90-foot swell. Now people are asking how big can it get? It's only a matter of time before we see an *el nino* storm big enough.'

First published in *Tracks* magazine, 2004.

15

NAT YOUNG'S DREAM

Just turned fifty, Nat holds court on Bob
Dylan, surfing as religion and why he
smokes pot with his kids

Tim Baker

Nat Young is leaning back in his lounge, eyes clenched, head
back, mouthing the words and fingering air guitar to 'Bob Dylan's
Dream'. 'That song,' he offers, 'tells the story of my life better
than anything.' I listen with new attention, trying to hear the
lyrics. Nat's son Beau, twenty-four, sitting next to him, observes
his dad with amusement. The plaintive, folksy ballad, as far as I
can work out, is the story of a man travelling west on a train,
falling asleep and having a dream. Bob's long, drawn-out warbles
are sometimes tricky to decipher, just like Nat's more esoteric,

stream of consciousness raves. There's something in there about youthful dreams, a kind of hippy idealism, that Nat reckons takes him back to what he calls his 'Eastern Suburbs' period, drinking good red wine and listening to lots of Bob Dylan. But there's a hint of sadness, too, that life turned out somehow harder, crueller, with more knocks and painful compromises, than those youthful hippies might have imagined.

Photographer Kidman and I are standing in the car park after a surf in fun three- to four-foot waves on the point, when Nat comes riding up the hill on his push-bike. 'Follow me,' he bawls playfully, resting his bike against a post and taking off on a narrow track through the bush down the hill. I give chase and can barely keep up through the twists and turns and overhanging branches. We come out to a small clearing and a rough wooden shack, fashioned out of branches tied together with wire and a palm frond roof, overlooking the point. It provides a fresh perspective of this famed break and serves immediately to ground me in my surroundings.

Nat's in an animated mood, just beyond his fiftieth birthday, on the eve of the publication of his autobiography, entitled, inevitably, *Nat's Nat and That's That*. He's just had the *Good Weekend* magazine people preparing a profile and is gearing up for the full media blitz.

We return to Nat's stylish home and holiday apartments overlooking Spookys and greet the family — wife Ti, fourteen-year-old daughter Nava, and eight-year-old son Bryce. His two other children, from his first marriage, Beau and Naomi, live in Sydney near their mother Marilyn. We've timed our trip to coincide with Beau paying his dad a visit for a few days. Beau's just shaped his first surfboard, a single fin based on the planshape of the board Nat rode in the seminal '70s surf movie *Morning of the Earth*, and Beau wants to ride it on those same, idyllic north coast waves Nat immortalised it on.

The imminent release of Nat's book dominates the household. 'I read the first chapter and couldn't read any more,' Nava tells me. Nat reckons he's spent more than he planned on the project and needs to sell a heap of books to return his investment. He jokes about giving away the surplus as Christmas presents for the rest of his life.

The family seem to be bracing themselves for one more blast of the public spotlight on their private lives. A Sydney *Sun Herald* newspaper article, on the occasion of Nat's fiftieth birthday, carried the banner headline, 'Nat Young has smoked pot with two of his children and plans to smoke pot with his youngest daughter.' Halfway through the story it's explained that when each of his children turns sixteen, Nat makes a tradition of sharing their first joint with them, so they experience it in a safe environment rather than experimenting on their own; but the headline alone was enough to raise a few hackles in these conservative country environs.

Nat has been telling us how he hasn't heard from his old mate Wayne Lynch for months, has left a dozen messages without response, and is wondering whether he's pissed off about something. Ten minutes later, with supernatural timing, the phone rings and it's Wayne, calling from Victoria. They rave for an hour, covering everything from the Midget feud to Peter Drouyn and Gerry Lopez's bit of biff at last year's Oxbow Masters, to the whole concept of Masters surfing and what form such an event should take. At the end of it all, Nat says simply, 'See ya. I love you.'

Nat sets us up in one of his handsome apartments (designed by old friend Paul Witzig and fashioned from timber milled at Nat's farm) and we settle easily into the Young routine — surfing on long and shortboards a couple of times a day, adjourning for Nat's obligatory 11am coffee, afternoon games of tennis, a counter tea at the pub, or Ti's magnificent home cooking. We borrow a bunch of his old videos — *Fantastic Plastic Machine*, *Fall Line*, and a copy of *Evolution* (which has been rented from the Evans Head video store for $3 a week, and never returned) — and set about immersing ourselves in the study of Natology. There is a surreal moment when we're watching Nat's opening spiel in *Fall Line* as he sits on his surfboard talking to camera, when the man himself walks through the door of our apartment and we glance back and forth at video Nat, age thirty, and real life Nat standing before us. 'Hah,' he bellows, 'I couldn't remember my lines and I had my notes sticky taped to the nose of my board.' We stop, rewind, play, pause, and there they are.

Throughout the video Nat surfs, mono-skis, jumps off cliffs and learns to hang-glide, apparently verging on disaster numerous times. 'He's Alby Mangels,' Kidman reckons, and we imagine a Nat action doll, complete with multiple accessories.

When we arrive at Nat's in the morning for a surf, he is almost invariably up in his office, on a mezzanine level that overlooks the living area and kitchen. His voice booms out like a godly pronouncement from above. It's pretty easy to allow yourself to get swept along in Nat's wake. He can be great fun to hang out with, though I suspect it must be a big job being Nat, constantly living up to the legend. A pair of Western Australian surfers on a round-Australia surfari knock on the door with a copy of his surfing guidebook, wanting him to autograph it and tell them where they might find waves. He happily indulges them and gives them detailed directions to a little known spot down the coast. 'I usually get one or two of them a day,' he reckons.

Beau arrives after a couple of days, having driven nine hours north from Sydney. He looks through the proofs of his dad's book and seems impressed. 'You've actually been doing something. That's not like you, Pops,' he teases.

We go for a surf at a nearby beachbreak, fun and punchy, wedging off a long rock groyne at four to five feet. Nat is riding his Rodney Dahlberg shortboard, a six-foot-six square tail. Rod gave him a bit of extra thickness in the latest one ('He's over fifty, after all,' Rod reasoned) and despite Nat's concerns it appears to work magically for him. He goes for one enormous vertical re-entry right over Kidman, as he bobs in the water taking photos, and nearly takes his head off. Nat falls out of the lip of the solid five-foot wave, lands it and surfs off down the line. 'Did you see that?' Beau shrieks with filial pride. 'That's the best turn I've seen him do in years.'

We surf for three hours with no more than two other surfers and have a ball. Beau rides the *Morning of the Earth* replica without a leggy and has a few swims, but manages to guide it through some impressive turns. After an hour or so he jumps on his normal shortboard and rips into the waves with grommet energy. 'All the longboarders think I'm a shortboarder and all the shortboarders think I'm a longboarder,' he tells us later. As with his dad, it seems a moot point to Beau, simply a matter of choosing the right equipment for the waves. Later that day, as the swell drops, Nat, Beau and Nava go for a late session at Spookys on longboards, sharing the tiny, rolling rows of foam as the setting sun bathes the picturesque bay in heavenly shades of red and orange. It feels almost intrusive to be in the water with them, like it's some holy family communion.

A couple of days later, as the swell drops, we surf the back beach, which is barely breaking out the back, filling up and slapping the shore in zippering close-outs. I'm the only one on a shortboard and I flounder, while the others have a blast on longboards. Nat's critical of a lot of modern longboards that try to incorporate new design trends, like an abrupt kick in the tail. 'If a longboard's got no flow, it's got nothing,' he says. I try to develop an appreciation for the subtle bottom curves of his and Beau's equipment and decide it's like trying to detect the bend in the horizon.

The fact that Nat ran away from home at fourteen to pursue the far-fetched notion of surfing for a living doesn't stop him worrying about his own children's career directions; and Beau, sponsored by French clothing label Oxbow, is subjected to much paternal chiding to 'get serious' about his life.

Nat today is a curious mix of old hippy, freedom-loving bohemian and pragmatic, at times almost redneck, country conservative. Politically, he's a Labor man through and through — has been since he donated his $600 prize money from the '74 Coke Surfabout to Gough Whitlam's election campaign. Yet, he'll express doubts about his local ALP candidate because she's a housewife who couldn't possibly understand 'the essence of Labor'. He'll curse 'the bloody Japs' who stuffed up a dishwasher in one of his apartments by putting a bar of soap where the detergent should go, and embrace gay literary luminary Patrick White as one of his 'absolute heroes'. He's big on heroes, who include, of course, Gough Whitlam, whose famous 'crash through or crash' style of politics seems to epitomise Nat's personal style too. That evening at the Sydney Opera House in '74, when he sat on stage alongside Gough and other Labor Party luminaries and supporters such as Tom Uren and Patrick White, had a profound effect on Nat. Kidman and I, leftist pinko sympathisers from way back, but who can barely recall the outrage of Gough's dismissal, are enthralled by Nat's recollections of the night.

'I got a little tongue-tied because I was slightly overwhelmed. I tried to just speak from the heart,' Nat says. 'I felt like I was a bit out of my depth . . . Basically I was surrounded by academics or people from the arts. I had a really good discussion with

Patrick White because the *Tree of Man* was one of the most influential books for me in my reading . . . The *Tree of Man* tells about a family growing and being taken over by a city — the few shacks on the edge of town turn into a big town which turns into a city — and it's sort of like a real mirror of what happened in Australia. And whether you could grow to be able to understand this and live with this, or whether it was going to absorb you and roll you . . . Patrick White was a very important person on that level.'

This unlikely pair discovered they had a connection that went back twenty-five years. 'He was living down at Werri at that stage, him and his boyfriend, and they were very much in love and they used to spend a lot of time walking on the beach. He said he used to watch surfing and watch waves. Werri, from my childhood, was very important because there was a golf club and it was abandoned and we used to go in and just stay there. And Patrick understood. He said, "Oh, we used to laugh about the way the golf club had turned into a derelict place and the surfers were squatting there on the weekends." So he knew exactly where my head was at.'

Where Nat's head has been at, of course, is an issue that occupies a giant place in our surfing history. Not content to simply let his surfing do the talking, Nat has always explained himself to the surfing public, through his own personal journey. Some call it grand egotism. I don't know. It often comes off as a genuine sense of filling some need of our surfing culture for leaders, orators and elders.

He matter-of-factly proclaims Makaha patriarch Buffalo Keaulana the one true Kahuna of world surfing. He goes on, 'We *need* to have a Kahuna. But everyone goes, well, what is it? IT'S A SURF GOD!' Nat very nearly roars, 'We need one, we're a different culture. We have different values. Buffalo — it's like that's his gift.'

Nat launches into a tale of Buffalo rescuing him at the '65 world titles in Peru, when Nat got a bit too drunk at the awards night. 'They were all trying to dress me in a tie and suit and stuff in the back of the Waikiki Club in Peru. And Buffalo just came and picked me up like a sack of potatoes and put me over his shoulder and took me out there and said, "On behalf of Nat Young I'd like to say aloha, and we're very pleased to be enjoying your country." And he just gave them all a look at me over his shoulder and then just walked off.'

As if to strengthen the case for Buffalo's appointment, Nat plunges into another story of Buffalo quelling hostilities between the surfing nations. 'The Hawaiians and Peruvians were at each other's throats, and there was this big meeting. George Downing and Eduardo Arena are screaming at each other. Buffalo just pulls a ukelele out and starts playing "Pearly Shells", and they're talking and Buff says, "I think best you quiet Georgie".'

At this point in the tale, Nat starts singing in a deep, Hawaiian voice, mimicking Buffalo, 'Pearly shells, pearly shells'. Nat continues: 'He sings and then he goes, "I think it best you sing with me, Georgie" and makes George sing "Pearly Shells" with him. And by the end of that thing, all of us, he gave each of our countries a turn to sing, "Pearly Shells". He reminded us that we were all together . . . And it just worked so well.'

The intervening years have been well documented. The glorious overthrow of the noseriders at the '66 world titles. The shortboard revolution. The country soul '70s. The growing entrepreneurial ventures in the '80s. Books. Films. The surf shop. Run-ins with police. Political aspirations. Plane crashes. The glorious sweep to victory in the new age of pro longboarding in the '80s.

Nat seems to have kept up a pretty frenetic pace, kind of like Madonna, always finding ways to reinvent himself, keep himself relevant to the wider surfing world. Except, that is, for the last few years of relative quiet, brought on by a serious snowboarding accident in the US five years ago. Coming down the mountain with Ti and Nava at the end of the day, he decided to go for one more run while his wife and daughter waited at the bottom for him. When he hadn't appeared after twenty minutes, Ti took the chairlift back to the top, skied down, and found him unconscious and bleeding from a major head wound next to a tree.

'The turnaround was the accident in Sun Valley,' Nat says simply. 'I was sick. I'd been hit very severely in the head and I actually had some brain damage, and so I was on heavy medication to try and get me back to a position to where I could think again.' He suffered shocking migraine headaches, had to give up air travel and working for the French clothing label, Oxbow.

Of course, a Nat interview wouldn't be complete without some discussion of his well-publicised drug dalliances. It's part of why we love him. Nat will talk about it all, break down taboos and conventions with the passion and bluster of his opinions. 'I never stuck a needle in me,' he declares at one point. 'The only time drugs ever consumed me was when I was grieving, living in Darlinghurst for six months.' Despite what the neighbours might think, there are no wild, drug-fuelled parties at the Young household these days. Ti is vehemently anti-drugs and Nat, apart from the occasional choof with old friends, doesn't touch the stuff. Still, he remains a passionate supporter of relaxing drug prohibition. 'Everybody says we've got to protect people from drugs,' Nat starts off. 'BULLSHIT! Give everybody as much drugs as they want. If they want to kill themselves, so what? All you're doing is taking people off the planet and leaving it to people who really want to live.'

Which brings us to Nat's abiding personal philosophy. 'Make it a beautiful life,' he declares bluntly, numerous times during our stay. 'You've got to make it a beautiful life 'cause if you don't there's no point. It's totally up to you.'

Is he religious, I wonder. 'My religion is the religion of surfing and nobody can tell me that what I do and everybody I know does, and what we did yesterday, is not a religious experience . . . When you practise something regularly, what you are doing is practising union with nature in order to become aware of the things that are important to you and the things that a lot of other like-minded people happen to believe.'

When a whole lot of us do this, Nat explains, we become a formidable vibration on planet earth, able to influence and inspire others, maybe even help save the planet. 'I feel very strongly that surfing has been underrated from the religious side,' says Nat. 'I think it's been sold very cheaply. It should have been sold as an artform . . . and people would have got away from the fucking winner thing, because this is what creates all the animosity . . . Why do we need a winner? I don't need a winner. Needing a winner is a very crude way to go.'

Those who have witnessed Nat in the midst of competitive fervour might be surprised by such ideals, but he is just getting warmed up. 'And the blame even goes back further than that, to the companies now, Billabong and Quiksilver; they're very strong in the world and those people know and understand. Greasy [Billabong boss, Gordon Merchant] is one of my neighbours here, a very good surfer, and understands absolutely that surfing's not a fucking sport — the same as Greeny, the guy that owns Quiksilver, understands that surfing's not just a sport. And they should make sure that the artistic end of it is covered more than the winner thing . . . that doesn't have to be the whole be-all and end-all. They should be trying to let surfing get stronger through artistic, religious connotations.'

I'd been a bit taken aback by the nostalgic melancholy of 'Bob Dylan's Dream', the sense that the idealistic fancies of youth will inevitably fade and slip through your fingers.

After a week at Nat's, though, I'm starting to get the idea that all those rose-coloured hippy days stand as a bit of a benchmark of how high and stoked on life you can be, which

Nat uses to this day as a reference point to keep him stoked. And if he's weathered the years a bit easier than old Bob, it's because he's a surfer.

'That's what's so nice about surfing,' Nat agrees. 'You have this continual thread. No matter how depressed you get on the beach — you go through all these problems associated with women or with children or with life in general — there's this thread, this unbelievable reality that you've got running through your life which I don't think a lot of people do. They talk about the despair out there, and I think surfers are so lucky to have this reality because it can stave off despair. We all got to ride unbelievable waves yesterday and that's always going to be there — that we had a really good day, just cruising and riding waves.'

First published in *Surfing World* magazine, 1998.

16

SPIDER

One afternoon of pumping waves with the local legend can make an entire grommethood

Sean Doherty

'Right here will be fine, Mum, we'll walk the rest of the way.'

My brother and I made Mum drop us around the corner. Pulling up in front of everyone at our local boardriders contest in a dork-green Volvo driven by your old duck was *beyond* uncool, especially in front of the older guys. I was fourteen, and at fourteen your whole world revolves around cool.

It was a sunny winter's morning, and the car park at Forster main beach resembled the set of *Mad Max II*. A dozen feral surfmobiles parked side by side, ranging from grubby work utes to patchwork-panel Datsuns to Kombis that belched smoke from both the exhaust pipe and the back seat. Milling around them were fifty suitably assorted surf-mad misfits, pacing impatiently at the prospect of a good day of waves. Milling around *them* were half a dozen dogs, all of whom were related somewhere within the past two generations. People from outside our town often said similar things about the place's human population.

The club president walked back from a nearby payphone (this was a good decade before surf checks were done with mobile phones) and announced that we'd be heading down the coast for today's contest. But before this depraved convoy could depart, twenty-odd grommets would first have to be billeted into cars for the trip. It was always a bit of a battle among us to try and get into one of the cool guys' cars. Grabbing a lift with my mate's old man in his shitbox-brown Nimbus just didn't cut it.

A gaggle of awkward, knock-kneed grommets in Oakley frogskins carrying Bob Brown surfboards in stripy fabric covers lined up waiting to be picked. The longer you got left the less fun your ride would be.

This particular day I was starting to worry, as the cool guys' cars were quickly being filled, when I heard, 'Doherty, you little bastard, get in. Bring ya brother with ya.'

We'd scored. Along with about ten other grommets, we were soon throwing our gear into the back of Buckets' white Kombi van. Buckets, a local ding repairer whose nickname apparently derived from the volume of his sexual output, stood a towering five-foot nothing, and looked like an extra from *Lord of the Rings*.

He was, however, the funniest, swearingest man we knew. The fact that he was forty, rode a mal and lived with his mum made his whole act seem even more hilarious.

The Kombi burned out of the car park — as much as a Kombi can burn out — and we were off. The first surf check was down a dirt road with a kilometre of undulating washouts creating the perfect opportunity for Buckets to put on a show for his captive audience. Despite being three times our age, he was still one of us at heart, and with a dozen grommets in the back his behavioural age regressed to that of a twelve-year-old.

We hit the dirt road at 70, and shit started flying everywhere. Boards, backpacks and grommets were pinballing off the Kombi's interior roof and panels and all the time we were pissing ourselves laughing . . . laughing so hard we didn't feel the pain shooting through our battered limbs. We later worked out that it was a deliberate ploy by Buckets to generate work. Our boards would be so dinged by the time we got there that Buckets would score a day's repair work out of it.

It turned out the surf was pretty good that day, and it was memorable for me for two reasons. The first of these was that I managed to beat Beau Emerton in the B-grade final. He was the local hotshot and would go on in later years to turn pro. It was the first time I'd ever beaten him; it took our head-to-head record to an inglorious 1–25. The fact that the judging panel for the final consisted of three of my mates didn't take any gloss off my win. Well, not for me, anyhow. I proceeded to give Beau heaps, too. Breaking the Beau Emerton hoodoo was a particularly

important stage in my surfing development. Unfortunately, he
was only nine then while I was fourteen and twice his size.

The second memorable thing happened just as the A-grade
final wound down. During the day there'd been a definite kick in
the swell. So much so that, combined with a low, turning tide,
speculation soon spread that our local river mouth back in town
might be firing. Three of us groms were sitting there, packed up
ready to go, when a skinny black shadow, stretched by the
sinking sun, descended over us from behind. Twisting around
simultaneously and squinting at the tall silhouette behind us, we
heard a soft, lulling voice. 'Hey, boys, The Bar'll be pumping.
Grab your stuff.'

We couldn't believe it. It was the six-foot-four (184-
centimetre) frame of legendary local shaper Steven 'Spider'
Spotsworth. Spider was a quiet, mysterious bloke, and a bloody
good surfer who enjoyed cult status among us grommets. No
sooner had he asked us than we'd overtaken him and were
waiting by his car — a metallic gold '75 Valiant station wagon
that looked like a hearse. As soon as we hit the road it felt like it
could become one at any minute.

Spider left the car park in a cloud of dust and a shower of
gravel. That was the last time the needle dropped below 100. On
a straight bit of road this may not be so much of a problem. But
we had to negotiate five kilometres of winding bends that had
recommended cornering speeds of 55. While the back of
Buckets' Kombi was fun, this was white-knuckle territory. Spider
had his window down and his big blond head was kind of

hanging out the window like a big skinny golden retriever. It was as if he was trying to smell surf. We looked at each other worriedly. I was jabbed in the ribs, and as senior grommet I was nominated to state our concerns.

'Umm, er, Spider, aren't we going a bit quick?'

He either didn't hear me over the roar of the Val or he was completely in the zone thinking about how good the surf was going to be, because he didn't answer. In fact, if anything he actually went quicker.

We got into town in one piece, and sure enough the surf was firing. Six foot, oily smooth, and breaking for longer than our legs could carry us. We surfed with Spider all afternoon. Just us and him. He directed us around the lineup like a traffic cop, told us where to sit, called us into a few . . . and I even saw him break out into a rare smile after one wave. It was the most animated we'd ever seen him, and it was clear he was having as good a time surfing with us as we were with him.

It was the last time we'd ever hang out with Spider because he dropped dead not long after. Walking over the dunes one day to his local beach at Tuncurry, Spider collapsed and that was it. Gone, leaving only his dog, his board, his Valiant, and memories that will live on in the minds of grommets like myself. During the eternity it took him to drop to the sand I'm sure he was wishing that this was all happening ten minutes later, out in the water. That's where he would have wanted to go out, but he probably figured the beach was the next best thing. And maybe, as his life flashed before him, there might have been a brief second when he remembered a classic afternoon surfing The Bar, just him and a bunch of young kids.

A few years later we moved away from Forster, and soon heard that our local boardriders club had folded. It has never been resurrected in the twenty years since. It was kind of sad, because our club had been like a family to us every fourth Sunday. Sure, there were any number of sketchy characters among its membership — fishermen, glassers, chippies, footballers, dope fiends — but once a month all the older guys would be like second fathers to us grommets, and they'd take that responsibility seriously. Guys like Spider. They made sure you'd never leave rubbish on the beach, always made you carry your share of club gear, always let you know when you'd surfed a good heat, and were quick to pull you into line if you started acting like a rooster. It was like one big semi-dysfunctional surfing Brady Bunch.

To this day I still go a bit white when I'm driving around those bends. And I think of Spider every time.

First published in *Tracks* magazine, 2002.

17

RETURN OF THE KING

King-hit outside a nightclub, one of Australia's top surfers battles to regain his balance, his hearing and his surfing

Matt Griggs

'People were trying to tell me how to feel. But they didn't have this fucking contraption in their ear making noises they couldn't understand. They didn't know what it's like not to have balance. I just had to get away . . . from everyone and everything.'

It's been sixteen weeks since one of the country's best surfers, Andy King, tasted death when a punch sent his skull crashing into the pavement. It's been thirteen weeks since he wobbled and staggered out of hospital minus his balance and hearing. It's been eleven weeks since learning how to walk again, nine weeks since learning how to surf again — and after a massive fundraiser to pay for bionic hearing, he is about to test-drive the cochlear implant that will enable him to once again hear. It's supposed to be one of Andy's first major steps towards getting his life back on track, and his family and girlfriend are there to help him. But the silence he once called 'bliss' has gone . . . forever. In its place are robotic voices giving unqualified advice. These voices are his family's — but he can no longer make out what's noise and what's human voice.

He freaks. After four months of getting incredible support, Andy realises he is once again alone. He splits down the coast, by himself, for a few days to try to get used to his new life and return to what was almost taken away — himself, and his surfing.

Sunday morning 2.30 am, Andy King decided to leave a Cronulla nightclub with his girlfriend and go home. Two minutes later his life changed, forever.

'I was just cruising home and this guy kept yelling out abuse at my girl,' Andy recalls. 'I didn't do anything — I guess he was a bit bitter because he didn't have a girl with him, but he just wouldn't stop yelling. So I went over, and apparently he threw a punch at me when I wasn't ready. But it wasn't the punch that did the damage. It was when the back of my head hit the pavement.'

Andy was out cold until the ambulance arrived, people at the scene beginning to get hysterical. After he was rushed to Sutherland Hospital, the doctors realised it was a very serious situation and by the next day, he was in the head injuries unit of

St George Hospital, in a critical condition. In fact he should have been dead. The x-rays showed a massive fracture running from the base of his skull around toward his ears. His hearing and balance were wrecked and he was freaking. If Andy rolled on his side he'd fall off the bed; if he coughed, he could haemorrhage due to the amount of swelling around his brain.

The doctors, looking at the x-ray, noticed something peculiar. Somehow, the fracture stopped at the major artery that feeds the brain with blood, leaving an air bubble, and then continued again in the bone, for a few more centimetres. How can a fracture that cracks the strongest bone in the body stop at an artery that feeds life to the brain, then start again on the other side? The doctors didn't get it. Messages were written so that Andy knew what was going on. But he feared they were keeping something from him — and in the silence engulfing him he feared the worst.

'I didn't know if I would die, if I'd ever walk again. My head felt like it was going to explode. There was so much pressure from the swelling that to even cough was dangerous. They told me I'd lost my hearing forever, but for some reason, that didn't bother me too much. I'd gladly exchange my hearing to be able to surf. But I couldn't get a straight answer from anyone. Those first few days were so hard.'

When this happened to my best friend I cried for a couple of days straight. I was down at Bells, and the memory of Richard Marsh and Nadine ringing me to explain what was happening still brings a tear to my eye. 'He's fractured his skull . . . he can't hear a thing . . . it doesn't look good . . .' It's amazing the tricks your mind plays on you in these situations.

Back in Sydney, I greet Nadine at the airport. We hug and don't let go until the tears die down a little. Arriving at the hospital, nervousness takes over — I'm half anxious and half scared about what I'm going to see. But as I walk through the door of Andy's room and see his smiling melon, things pick up. Andy doesn't have a broken face, there's no black eye. The damage is inside, but it's only physical. On the outside there's my best mate, as proud as ever, as funny as ever. He doesn't want anyone to worry about him; he's doing enough of that himself.

We converse for around five minutes, just talking shit, about who won Bells, who ripped . . . Unbeknown to us, Andy's sisters, mum and Nadine are watching in disbelief as Andy shows the first signs of a new skill — lip-reading. He looks around the place he'll call home for the next three weeks. Beside him is an overweight beast who can't fit in his bed. Across the hall, past the bad hospital smell, is an old man who has given up on life. But next to *me* is someone who is beginning a new one.

Andy's rehabilitation started when he got home, along with plans to get him a cochlear implant — a new technology that would help him to hear again. 'Once I knew what I needed to do,' he said about the rehab, 'I knew I'd be fine. I just had to be given the work. The worst thing was not knowing.' All along, Andy was never a victim. He never thought 'What if?' He only thought 'What now?' He didn't want to be fussed over, because it would remind him of what he didn't want to be — handicapped. He approached the job at hand as he'd approached life as a professional surfer — with simple hard work and born of desire. His rehab in the early days basically involved trying to stay on his feet while looking around the room. He would do it, re-do it, and re-do it again.

Meanwhile, friends were getting together to help out. Richard Marsh, Mark Aprolovic, Mark MacCarthy and I were quickly joined by people like Kelly Slater, Occy, Parko, Fanning, Kostya Tszyu and Andrew Johns. We had people everywhere ringing up and offering everything from surfboards to footy jumpers to help with raising money. The fundraising campaign was not only to pay for a cochlear implant, but also to give Andy time to get settled without the stress of paying rent. We organised a charity golf day, a surfing event and a sporting auction.

Four weeks after the accident, Andy is starting to walk again. 'It's hard,' he tells me, as we move slowly out on the sand dunes with pro surfer Nathan Hedge. The track is windy, and so is Andy's stride. As he looks at me, he almost falls. 'It's hard for me to walk and talk, because I have to watch where I'm putting my feet, or I'll fall.' Andy follows Hog and me up and down the sand dunes for a training session. He snakes his way along the track as if drunk. But he never loses his focus, his temper or his commitment.

'When you have these things taken from you, you realise what's important,' says Andy. 'When I was stuck in hospital and couldn't move, I realised how unreal it feels to be fit and strong. My health, friends and surfing are everything. I don't care if I never hear again. I have to get my balance back . . . I have to surf.'

Five weeks later, he is.

After twelve years of chasing big waves together at home and around the world, I find myself walking slowly down the beach with Andy towards a two-foot left-hander at our local beachbreak. Andy is wearing a life jacket, and looking at the waves with uncertainty. He is learning how to surf — all over again.

On entering the salt water, he screams with joy — 'This is unreal!' Everyone wonders where the noise is coming from, but Andy can't hear it (he talks loudly at this stage because without the vibrations from almost yelling, he isn't sure if he is finishing sentences).

'Is this a wave?' Andy shouts. Without equilibrium, things tend to rush past him and he can't make them out. He paddles with the timing of a beginner and stands up, attempting to ride across the wave. But, without balance, he comes unstuck as soon as the wave changes shape. He falls. He then rises to the surface with the aid of the life jacket, but as he does so, he starts swimming back down in a panic. Fuck! He doesn't know which way is up. I swim frantically towards Andy as he slaps helplessly at the water. It's a scary moment, and he should come in right now. But he doesn't. He shouldn't even be in the water, but he is. If Andy had listened to the doctor's advice, he'd be sitting on a couch feeling sorry for himself. But he's not! Anyone who knows Andy knows that his whole life revolves around the ocean.

After a few surfs, we learn that the only way to do it is not to swim but to actually lie still and trust the buoyancy of the life jacket. After two weeks of rehab, surfing, swimming and lung-capacity work, Andy is finding things in his mind and body he never knew he had. When he leans his head to the right, it doesn't feel any different from when it is centred, so he is working out new ways to achieve balance. He is adapting steadily and he soon decides that he is ready to take on Voodoo, a powerful local reef break on which he usually reigns supreme. It's a special moment. I ride the first (four-foot) wave behind him and watch as he feels his way up and down the face of it like a blind man reading Braille. He screams, hoots and smiles for ages before finally kicking out. 'I feel like I just got a 20-foot barrel at Pipe,' he yells, his face lit up in excitement. Andy has got barrelled at 20-foot Pipe, so the comparison is well credentialed — and now, going straight on his favourite wave is enough to send him into ecstasy. Out the back, he sits wide, looks to the ocean, and smiles. It's as if someone has just told him a joke — and he doesn't stop laughing for the rest of the surf. He can't hear the surf, but he sure can feel it.

Nine weeks later, the fundraiser was just days away. Last minute preparations are being made — and half the WCT (World Championship Tour) had arrived in Cronulla. Kelly Slater, Occy,

Parko, Fanning, Dean Morrison, Kieren Perrow, Richie Lovett...

Andy found himself in the first heat with his childhood hero, Mark Occhilupo. He surfed a spirited heat and, when he came in, was clapped by all the local grommets at the water's edge and hugged by his closest friends. And for the first time since the accident happened, Andy broke down. He later recalled, 'It was too much. I hadn't cried once and it was like everything came together and I just put on the waterworks.'

The comp was eventually won by Central Coast surfer Dave Nielson, with Perrow, Occy and Deano also making the final.

The auction followed that night. Kelly had donated a board and it went for $6500. In addition, Fanning, Parko, Dean Morrison and the makers of 3 Degrees (Matt Gye and Shagga) donated $10 000 from their video profits. By the end of the night, $90 000 had been made. Combined with the golf day, all the donations and the raffles and so on we had around $120 000.

After a hectic, exhilarating week, Andy's friends returned to their normal lives. Andy, still in silence, was readying himself for his operation. 'I just got my first proper barrel at Vooie,' he texted me while I was at J-Bay the day before the operation. 'I'm training every day. I'm so tough right now, Dr Chang won't be able to cut me.'

The next day the doctor would cut his head open and insert the cochlear implant at the point where his hearing and balance systems had fractured. He would have to endure a couple of surfless weeks, until the wound healed, then have an outside hearing aid attached. At this stage, all Andy was concerned about was having to be out of the water.

The silence was never a problem for him. 'Nobody's ever got anything good to say, anyway,' he maintained with a laugh. But after a successful operation, Andy found himself, literally, about to get switched on. His girl, his mum and his sisters were there to help celebrate the event.

But sound had become for Andy a kind of weird robotic noise. Planes going overhead sounded like kitchen blenders. And he didn't know if that was his girl trying to tell him that everything would be all right, or 'a chipmunk on acid.'

He freaked. Needing to be alone, he went off to the south coast of New South Wales for a few days. After some good surfs down there, he came back with a smile, ready to take on a new challenge.

Andy still wants to qualify for the World Championship Tour. At the moment, he is working at about 80 per cent of his normal ability. He is starting to commit to his turns a lot harder and even connecting them. 'I'm not as scared to fall off now,' he says. 'I know I'll float up eventually, so I'm kinda going for it a bit more. It's amazing how your body adjusts. Like, I don't have any balance fluid in my ears, so I can only balance by using my eyes and by touching the ground or my board with my feet. It's hard, but you get used to it.' On a normal day, Andy does yoga and his rehab, surfs and goes to the gym. When he's not at the gym, he's running sand dunes. And he does it all now with an appreciation of good health that most of us take for granted.

'It doesn't matter any more, y' know. I used to get caught up in trying too hard. I never really stopped to appreciate how good life is. Now, just being in the water makes me so happy. I don't feel bad about what happened and I don't feel like a handicapped person. I feel normal . . . I feel unreal, actually!'

Sixteen weeks later that smile is still there. His surfing is almost as good as it was, but his enjoyment is greater than ever. It's contagious. 'Look at his head,' I say to Richard Marsh, as we surf Voodoo one afternoon with just the three of us out. We are not scared any more as we watch him. We are watching him rip, proud of everything he has worked so hard for. I paddle over to him and manage to let him know that he is improving really quickly. 'You ain't seen nothing yet,' he yells back. He isn't thinking of all the bad things that have happened. He isn't thinking of all the work ahead of him if he's to attempt a comeback. He is simply looking at the ocean, smiling.

First published in *Tracks* magazine, 2004.

18

AFTER THE GOLDRUSH

When the contests, cameras and sponsors have gone home, who's left in Hawaii simply to go surfing?

Tim Baker

The thing I love about Hawaii — apart from the thrilling surf and tropical sunsets and rich watermanly culture — is the fact that here you can consume a tub of Haagen Dazs icecream and a six pack of beer a day and still not get fat. Diabetic or alcoholic perhaps, but certainly not fat.

Is it just me, or has anyone else ever noticed how big your poos are in Hawaii? Like you are literally shitting bricks. Life's processes seem somehow heightened here. Humans, vegetation, even cars and houses seem pulled into the exaggerated cycles of growth and decay, as if it will all just end up as so much compost. 'The quickening,' North Shore veteran Robbie Page calls it, an accelerating of all bodily functions — heartbeat, breathing, metabolism, adrenal glands, fight or flight reflexes — that lets you know very quickly how your physical state is holding up to the relentless pounding from the Pacific. It's like going to the doctor for your annual checkup to find out what kind of condition your heart, lungs and nervous system are in.

Somehow, it was six years since I'd been here. How the hell did that happen? A run-in with an aggrieved local, mortgage, marriage, child, no free air tickets forthcoming from obliging editors. This apparently random combination of elements had conspired to keep me away from surfing's spiritual home for too long. It was now or never, I figured, before middle-age crept up and handed me a beer gut and a longboard. My mission (apart from not drowning) was to document the late season, long after the contests, pro surfers and media hordes had packed up and gone home — to depict the North Shore in its natural state, and recognise those hardy souls who surf the entire season for simple love. In an age when the surf media focus has narrowed to a four-week window in contest season, and fly away airs at Rocky Point earn more publicity than any maxed-out Sunset heroics, surfing the North Shore in February is hardly a career move.

This noble pilgrimage would get to the heart of Hawaiian surfing and the unsung characters who brave its regularly life-threatening waves for no fanfare or reward. The island and the elements would thus assist my passage, open up and reveal themselves in a depth and richness denied the great media stampede of December. But if I was looking for divine intervention, perhaps I had come to the wrong place.

I was fearing for my life before I'd even set foot on Oahu's rich red volcanic soil. Our plane was hit by lightning as we circled Honolulu around midnight, waiting for a break in the storm to let us land. A huge flash of light and an enormous crack of thunder simultaneously shook and illuminated our little flying tin can. On the ground, they interrupted TV shows to broadcast severe storm warnings. Roofs blew off houses and trees fell across roads. The turnoff to the North Shore was blocked by one enormous toppled trunk and a police car, with its lights flashing, redirecting traffic. I was beginning to feel spooked, like someone or something was trying to discourage my visit. Were the gods displeased at my return? What would I find? How had it changed?

Well, the first thing — and I can't believe no one told me, or organised a mass protest — is that the classic old landmark orange lifeguard towers are gone, replaced by shiny, new, pale, spew-green plastic ones. They squat low to the ground like Apollo spacecraft and blend in with the green foliage behind, where the old, tall and proud orange ones stood out like beacons. I find myself feeling oddly upset. Hopefully, I won't need rescuing today anyway — it is mercifully small, onshore, grey, as I crawl out of the Backpackers, bleary-eyed and disoriented.

It feels amazing to jump in the water. I swear, the ocean here is alive, grabbing at your arms with each paddle like thick treacle, trying to pull you down into the deep. You can almost feel yourself becoming fitter, lungs expanding, muscles toning. The first person I see in the lineup is none other than ex-world champ Barton Lynch riding a nine-foot-six single fin switch foot at six-foot Sunset. BL's clocked up two decades of North Shore winters and along the way has quietly morphed from ruthless contest machine to soulful salty sea-dog. A small beach house at Backyards is one of the few remaining spoils of his pro tour glory days. 'I feel more comfortable here than I do at home,' he reckons.

Now a part-time surf coach, Barton still herds a bunch of his young charges over here each year to blood them in the serious business of North Shore survival. BL's young mate, WQS campaigner Beau Mitchell, is laid up on the couch with a stuffed shoulder, but is still stoked with his month in the islands. 'There hasn't been a wave over two feet at home and here it's hardly been under ten feet for a month,' he enthuses.

On land, the usual suspects inevitably bob up. Ross Clarke-Jones and tow-in partner Tony Ray are both out of action with injuries at the same time, for the first time in their careers. Ross speared himself with his board in a pinched death barrel at Jaws, and managed to crack a rib even through his life jacket. T. Ray met a similar fate at mid-sized Sunset, and copped stitches to his thigh. Ross is considering cortisone shots to get him out there if the swell comes up. All it takes is one massive wave caught on film to earn his salary for another year.

Kelly Slater's still here too. I spot him one grey late afternoon, streaking through almost unmakeable barrels in that gleaming white springsuit at six- to eight-foot Haleiwa. 'Whoa! Look at Kelly. Look at Kelly,' one enormous Hawaiian man bellows from the beach, as the White Knight claws his way into a collapsing tube on takeoff, disappears in a storm of whitewater, and somehow reappears at the base of the foamball as the wave shuts down over the shallow inside reef. The local crew are gathered round a picnic table and look up to admire the six-time world champ in action. There's not a photographer in sight. Eventually, Kelly's seven-foot pintail washes in, the legrope plug ripped clean out of the deck, and he wades in after it. How have the waves been, I ask. I've heard a chorus of complaints that the winds have been flukey. 'I like the different winds, because you surf all different places,' Kelly reasons. He looks keen and fit and in his element, hardly the wounded world title casualty he's been depicted.

As the sun sets over Kaena Point I score one of those sessions, with about a dozen mainly older local crew in the water, and hoots and laughs and a sublime vibe that even extends to unsteady, jetlagged *haole* hacks. Surrounded by superbly fit fifty-something Hawaiians charging solid double and triple overhead reef waves, it's easy to imagine your surfing future stretching out ahead of you indefinitely. Pro tour use-by dates and surf media youth fixations seem irrelevant here. That's why so many of the pro tour old boys club seem to cling to the place so keenly, I figure. I watch BL sitting out the back at Sunset one afternoon, happily chatting to North Shore pioneers Pete Cole and Steve Bigler and a bunch of other blokes twenty or thirty years BL's senior, and all of a sudden he's looking like a grommet.

Another day at Haleiwa I spot the truly legendary Ben Aipa charging solid eight-foot waves on an enormous ten-foot longboard, complete with his trademark stingers and swallowtail, fitted with curved outside fins, and belting the lip like his life depended on it. Here's a proud local, sixty-two years of age, who's traded waves with every great Hawaiian surfer from Eddie Aikau to Dane Kealoha, Sunny Garcia to Andy and Bruce Irons. He didn't start surfing until he was twenty-three, yet made the national team two years later. As a surfer, shaper and coach — a guy who's revolutionised equipment, surfing styles and competitive strategies — few can rival his wide-ranging influence and heavy rep. Yet he's friendly, approachable, keen for a chat, still surfing whenever it's on and heading into the shaping bay every day to carve more foam. He's just been diagnosed with diabetes, he tells me seriously, adding, 'That's my next challenge.' We arrange to do an interview. When I call him at his small shaping factory in town he answers the phone with 'How's the waves?' before he even asks who it is. Nice to think you can keep it that fresh for that long.

His shaping bay walls are covered with thank yous and testimonials from guys like Brad Gerlach and Sunny. 'Thanks for getting me psyched,' Bruce Irons has scrawled on a poster of himself at Pipe.

After another Haleiwa session, I get chatting to a thin, blond bloke named Shaun, a South African, with a wispy beard and a gleam in his eye. He's got a bloodied shin and has been riding a minuscule six-foot-one in up to eight-foot surf. He creased his seven-foot-four yesterday in a barrel at Sunset, he says. Shaun's doing the full North Shore poverty grovel. He's been sleeping under the church, but has borrowed a tent from someone and just needs somewhere to pitch it now. He's got his eye on a battered second-hand gun for $15 that he reckons he can patch up and make rideable. 'The waves are so perfect, you don't need a good board here. You've just got to take off and set up the barrel,' he reasons.

This is supposed to be the non-contest season, after the madness of December, yet during my two-week visit there are no fewer than three events on the North Shore — a piddling one star WQS that nevertheless monopolises Sunset for four or five days; the Pipe Bodysurfing comp; and the Backdoor Shootout. No wonder the locals get testy. Kelly only decides to enter the Sunset comp at the last minute, having pulled up to check the surf and been told there's a spare heat going out in a few minutes if he wants to pull on a coloured jersey. So he blazes all over mid-range Sunset all the way to the final, but is denied a win by Pancho Sullivan, playing like a big happy kid in his backyard. Sponger Mike Stewart wins the Bodysurfing comp, proving his all round watermanliness yet again. I can't tell you who wins the Shootout. I go to watch it one day and it's literally two to ten feet and can be dead flat for fifteen minutes, not a wave breaking. You could have run back and got your six-foot-two and paddled out for a grovel. The Volcom house, though, is typically rowdy, and way down at Off The Wall a bodyboarder accidentally drops in on one of their boys. The infamous whistle goes and I split rather than witness the repercussions.

Up at Sunset, a totally different variety of North Shore surfers settle their disputes in a very different manner. I'm told the tale of a large mainlander who has been dropping in and abusing everyone he comes across in the lineup. When he's inspired them to violence, he paddles in, goes to the police and gets a restraining order slapped against them. He's trying to take out the whole lineup, it seems, so he can surf it by himself. He's convinced he's one of the great Sunset surfers of all time, yet he rides with a theatrical, hood ornament type of posturing, with that classic American self-belief that he is actually killing it. A bunch of older locals get together and all slap restraining orders on *him*, making it impossible for him to surf Sunset when any of them are out. The litigious US at its finest. I'm not sure which way of dealing with drop-ins — the Pipe vigilantes or the Sunset litigators — I find more disturbing.

Here on the North Shore you can pick your favourite loon and, guaranteed, you'll start running in to them wherever you go. I'm torn between the buxom bodyboard lady with the boob job who raves to anyone who'll listen in the lineup or the car park, and the truly classic Sunset bike path sweepers. The latter are two wizened old North Shore vets of indeterminate age, who have taken it upon themselves to keep the Sunset bike track clear of beach sand. As one can imagine, this is very nearly a full-time job. Yet they expect no payment for this civic duty. They simply turn up at Sunset each morning with their brooms, install themselves at opposite ends of the bike path, and jump into action whenever any errant sand makes its way on to the fine bitumen path. In from a late surf at Kammies one afternoon, I run into one of them. He's cheery and chatty, sweeping away the last grains of the day, and keen to know how the waves are. 'You right for something to smoke?' he asks me, a complete stranger. I'm touched by his kindness but decline the offer.

The bodyboard lady gets my vote, however, for a wonderful tale I hear about her finding herself out the back of massive, closing-out Sunset with a certain former Australian pro surfer, some years ago. Bodyboard lady has recently had her breasts augmented, and as 15-foot bombs detonate all round them, and the rest of the lineup is washed in to the beach, she asks our pro surfer boy if he would like to inspect her new appendages. She is a stripper by trade and so this is an offer that usually comes at a price, but in the circumstances she's gonna make it a freebie. She even offers him a feel. The image of pro surfer boy manipulating the newly pneumatic breasts of bodyboard lady out the back of maxed-out Sunset is one not easily shaken from the consciousness.

I'm looking for a room to rent. I join the drifters hovering round the Foodland noticeboard. I see one advertised down by Alligators and go to check it out. Just as I pull up, a weathered old surfer-looking dude, somewhere either side of fifty, wanders out of the driveway to a dilapidated van and I approach him. He generously offers to share his thick, stubby little roll-your-own ciggie and before I know it, quite inexplicably, we seem to be cocooned in a warm fuzzy green cardigan of friendship. It's not *his* house — he's living in his van right now. The back of it is a mass of scattered clothes and belongings strewn over a stained foam mattress. He tells me stories about surfing with Pat Curren in the '60s. He'd be a thoroughly unique, wonderfully eccentric figure anywhere else in the world, like Harry Dean Stanton's character in *Paris, Texas*, except that the North Shore seems to be inhabited by hundreds of these guys. There's that warm acceptance, displayed by a lot of the older hobo types a little down on their luck, that embraces any human as a potential companion. He tells me to tell the owner of the house he's my friend. He drives off, I ring the bell on the gate and an enormous rottweiler announces its intention to dismember me. A woman comes out, forty or fifty something, kind of guarded. She asks what kind of rent I want to pay. I suggest US$250 a week, kind of at the low end of market rates, I figure. 'Watch out,' she warns me firmly. 'For that kind of money you're going to end up in drug houses.'

You forget sometimes this is the fiftieth state of the good ol' US of A, until you find yourself at the checkout at Foodland, reading the front page headline of *Weekly World News*: 'Saddam wins US Lottery weeks after his capture. It's only $100 but it will buy him a cigar and a bimbo.' Really? Or turn on the TV and discover some surreal reality TV share-house debacle featuring '80s white rap star Vanilla Ice, ex-porn star king Ron Jeremy and the Hispanic motorcycle cop from 'CHiPs'. Some teen-popstar type girlie is getting sloshed on white wine and hitting on Vanilla, who fends her off with stoic pronouncements that he loves his wife and kids, at which she decides Ice Baby is an 'asshole' and kindly Porn Ron tries to put her to bed like a caring, creepy uncle.

Then you go outside for a small lazy later-afternoon sesh and the Logs to Sunset stretch is like seven miles of small fun D-Bah and a good proportion of the island's inhabitants are peppered along the peaky fun park on all manner of surfcraft in perfect, harmonious aquatic bliss. It all resembles one of those etchings produced by the early European explorers when they first came upon the carefree Hawaiians merrily cavorting in their ocean playground. It is the only place I've seen bodysurfers call people off waves and get taken seriously. Families are having barbecues in the beach parks and there are those inflatable jumping castles everywhere and it seems like you'd have trouble getting a gruff word out of anyone on such a blessed afternoon. Even the black, jacked-up monster trucks look kind of comical, like some Noddy and Big Ears toy-land.

I come in from one such joyous session and bump into Noah Johnson on the beach in the fading light. He's just proven himself as adept in these skate ramp peaks as any outer reef cloudbreak. 'Smiles all round,' he beams. And he's right. Noah is one of those classic North Shore locals who has evolved from hot rat new schooler to serious charger over the space of a decade of quiet commitment.

'They keep calling 20-foot swells and they're only 15,' he complains, though I find it hard to share his disappointment.

You can drive across the historic Haleiwa bridge and see a crew of young golden-skinned Hawaiians launching their outrigger canoes for an arvo paddle out through the harbour. And against the setting sun and the majestic Kaena Point backdrop it could be precisely any time in the last millennium, when the local folk have been doing the exact same thing.

I check small Pipe at dawn one day, barely light and apparently four or five feet. Two bodyboarders scamper out in the crisp greyness. A guy in the car park has checked the buoys and tells me it's on the rise, to a predicted six to eight feet, with the odd ten. I'm terrified of this stretch of beach over head height, but I figure if I'm ever going to surf Pipe by myself on a rising swell, this is it. It's super clean and ridiculously fun — for about five minutes. That's the time it takes for about thirty bodyboarders to stream out from every little right of way to the beach like rows of ants and to infest the lineup. I am the only person on a surfboard. It is oddly unsettling being so outnumbered by our prone, flippered cousins and eventually I retreat to the beach on an inconsequential right in the face of the unremitting invasion.

Small Pipe is a hilarious spectacle. On another mellow day, I duck out for a couple and there is a large, helmeted American issuing stern commands like a sergeant major in the heat of battle — with a tone of urgency that seems to say, 'We are all in this together and if we stick together, well, hell, we might just make it.'

'Outside set,' he bellows as a rare four-footer looms on the reef.

'Wide one,' he hollers at a pack of startled boogers.

'Right, right, go right,' he orders a hapless grom.

And all the time firmly convinced he's engaged in a Serious Ocean Adventure Of The Highest Order.

You could expire from exhaustion while trying to document all the wonderful varieties of human strangeness on the North Shore — the unfailingly polite Japanese who have the neatest surfer households on earth, the cultlike Brazilian rasta crew camping behind the Taste of Paradise food van at Rocky Point, the bike path sweepers, the GIs, the tourists in buses and stretch limos who look at you admiringly like a superhero as you stride out of the Sunset shorebreak, even if you didn't manage to catch a wave, the heavy locals who can make you break out in a cold sweat with just a glance.

Despite the relentless overcrowding and exploitation, there is still much to admire about the North Shore and the resilience of its surf culture — the way anyone will stick a stray board up in the sand when it washes in, so you can see it as you swim in, the camaraderie that can still sprout up in random sessions that exude all the old aloha, the unfailing good humour of the lifeguards who quietly caretake the whole insane carnage, the simple acts of kindness of virtual strangers offering to lend you a board or a legrope because they don't want you to miss out on a surf.

No shit can stick to the North Shore. You can plaster your surf brand stickers all over your quivers of boards on the road signs, you can erect the biggest contest structures and banners in history, you can build the most ostentatious beachfront palaces — but in time the ocean will wipe it all away. Nothing lasts here except the all-conquering might of the ocean — and perhaps the spirits of those hardy souls who most closely align their lives with its rhythms.

Hawaii is our temple. Sure, there are moneylenders at the gate, tramps and hobos, prostitutes and conmen loitering around its steps. But get to the heart of it, out at sea, sitting astride a bigger board than you've ever ridden, swinging the nose around to point you shoreward at the approach of a cresting set, not knowing whether to catch the thing or try and dodge it, whether to paddle out to sea or back to the beach or cry like a baby, and you will know what it is to be truly alone with yourself.

My last surf at Sunset. The swell's coming up fast as the sun goes down. It's big and scary and crowded and the pack is neatly split in two — into the hunters and the hunted, as Gary Elkerton once succinctly put it. I watch in awe those surfers who stroke past me frothing, into a watery version of the running of the bulls, ready to meet the might of the ocean head on, and marvel at the idea of all the surfers who have come here over the decades and pushed themselves across that line. Simply, that journey of only one hundred metres or so, from Sunset's shoulder to its peak, is still the greatest test of a surfer.

First published in *Surfing Life* magazine, 2004.

19

THE LAST DAYS OF MIKI DORA

Surfing's black knight, the original rebel soul surfer, couldn't avoid exploitation even in death

Phil Jarratt

About two weeks after Miki Dora's death on 3 January 2002, I received a phone call just as I was leaving Australia to return to my job in France. Would I help sift through my neighbour's belongings and catalogue his papers and photographs of historical significance?

Of course, the answer was yes. Having spent a sizeable part of my life trying to unravel the mysterious personas of leading surfers around the world, I was hardly going to say no to an opportunity to pry into the affairs of the most mysterious of all surfers, the enigmatic Miklos Sandor Dora III. Once described as 'the most relentlessly committed soul surfer of all time', Miki had barely worked a day in his life. He had never won a surfing contest of note — in fact he'd shunned them most of his, er, career — and yet since he rose to prominence with the surf boom of the early 1960s he had been famous the world over as the quintessential surf outlaw, a role model for an entire generation of boys who just wanted to have fun.

But there was a catch. In his final years Miki and I had become friends, and I knew as well as anybody that journalistic opportunity had to be weighed against the privacy of a man who had spent much of his life in supposed paranoid retreat from public exposure. It was OK, I decided. I could peek into the private papers, as long as anything I concluded from them, and subsequently wrote about, was true to the spirit of the Miki Dora that I, and others closer to him in his final days, knew.

He was born on 11 August 1934 in Budapest, Hungary, the first child of wine merchant Miklos Dora Jr and his beautiful young wife, Ramona Stancliff Dora. At twenty-one, Miklos had already established a business career, but Ramona was just seventeen.

By March 1935, the Doras had relocated to California, living first in Pasadena, but the move turned out to be the beginning of the end of the marriage. By the beginning of the 1940s, Ramona had left Miklos and taken up with Gard Chapin, a surfer from Palos Verdes. Chapin was big, strong and handsome in a 1930s matinee-idol kind of way, which was fortunate since his ambition was to become a matinee idol. But while he knocked around the fringes of Hollywood without a lot of success, he enjoyed much greater fame through surfing. As well as being acknowledged as the best surfer in the South Bay, Chapin was a pioneer in surfboard design, creating revolutionary turned-down rail, nose-rocker models in his garage.

When he returned from his war service, Chapin started taking eleven-year-old Miki down the coast to San Onofre to surf. Now known as Mickey Chapin, the little kid with the lazy smile learnt bad surf manners from the master. Gard Chapin was loud, arrogant and abusive to anyone who got in his way. Wherever he surfed, from San O to Malibu, he was disliked with an intensity that can't have been lost on the little boy. So this was surfing — kind of like war. Take no prisoners, watch your back, trust no one.

But if Chapin was loathed by his surfing peers, he was idolised by Miki. Chapin made him a cut-down version of the board he rode, but it was so heavy that Miki could barely turn it. Then one day at Malibu, Chapin saw shaper Joe Quigg riding a relatively small, light pintail design. He badgered Quigg all afternoon until he agreed to sell it, and Chapin brought it home for Miki, who would remember it for most of his life as the 'best board ever'.

Ramona's relationship with Gard Chapin was volatile and needed more space than a young child allowed, so as soon as he was old enough, Miki was packed off to the first of a succession of military prep schools. But not all his schooling was private. For a time he attended Hollywood High, trading locker-room jokes with the brats of the stars. Only months before he died, I introduced Miki at a surfing legends dinner in Australia as 'surfing's answer to James Dean'. Afterwards he came up to me looking agitated. I got in ahead of him. 'I hope you didn't mind me introducing you up there,' I said.

'Introducing's fine,' Miki said, 'but don't you ever mention me in the same breath as James Dean. I went to Hollywood High with that faggot!'

While Miki was still in school, Gard Chapin disappeared from a yacht moored in a bay in Cabo San Lucas. His bloated body was fished out of the water some days later. There were conflicting versions of what had transpired, but for Miki there was only one explanation. 'My stepfather was murdered,' he would often say. He would let the words hang in the air, and hint at some broader conspiracy that endangered his life too.

So when the teenaged Mickey Chapin Dora emerged at Malibu at the dawn of the 1950s, he was part Gard, part Jimmy Dean (certainly not that part!) and all style. The contradictions that were to define him were already evident in every sly smirk and extravagant hand jive and in his defensive body language. No one could understand him, but everyone wanted to be just like him.

I first met Miki Dora in Bali in July or August 1975, about ten years after I had become aware of who he was through his black-hatted villain roles at Malibu in the early surf movies. (It was also about three months after he had skipped bail on fraud charges in the States, but I knew nothing of that.) I was a fan of the proto-punk Da Cat ads in the magazines too. Dora wasn't exactly a hero to me, but I found his persona endlessly fascinating. I was lying on my bunk reading after a morning session at Uluwatu in Bali when film-maker Jack McCoy pulled up on his motorcycle outside my room at Arena Bungalows in Kuta.

'Dora's waiting for us at the Legian Beach Hotel. You do the words and I'll take the photos.' I was on the back of the bike in a nanosecond. I'd heard on the grapevine that the great man was in Bali, but I'd also heard that he didn't give interviews. Christ, if he actually spoke to you, you'd been blessed!

McCoy rode down the back lanes and across the rice fields and paddocks, which are now all hideous Tommy Soeharto-owned concrete box hotels, and into the grounds of the hotel, which was then one of the more pleasant hideaways in Bali. He halted the Suzi 175 in front of a well-shaded bungalow and we climbed the steps to the tiny concrete porch with a cane table, a single chair, a plate with a couple of bananas on it, and a flask of tea. McCoy called out and a husky voice from within bade us enter. The small room was shuttered and very dark. A ceiling fan creaked slowly and I could just make out the figure of a deeply tanned, unshaven man sprawled on the bed. Dora, whose eyes had become accustomed to the darkness, could obviously see me quite well.

'What's that — a fucking tape recorder?' he growled. I was the one holding the offending object but the steely gaze and the question were directed at McCoy.

'This is Jarratt, from *Tracks*. The guy I was telling you about. It's OK, Miki, he's cool.' Jack kind of let the words hang in the air, while Miki nodded and made little grunts. When he spoke again it was in a hoarse whisper.

'No tape recorder, no pictures. I don't do interviews.'

I said, 'No problem. Jack said you were cool to just chat.' McCoy nodded profusely as backup. Miki didn't say any more but he seemed to accept his fate as McCoy took up a position on the floor under the fan and I claimed the only chair, by the shuttered window. The King of Malibu sighed deeply and started talking in riddles.

Two hours later McCoy and I emerged blinking in the light. As we got back on the bike, McCoy said, 'Is that guy a trip or what? Man, he's so on!' I smiled, shaking my head in wonderment, and asked McCoy to drop me at the sugar cane juice bar on Jalan Sari. With a long juice in front of me I sat at a rickety table and wrote, in a small, spiral-bound notebook, every word I could remember Dora saying. When I was done, I read and reread the gibberish, cutting bits here and there if I couldn't make sense of them. What I ended up with was a fascinating, stream-of-consciousness rave coming from a self-obsessed but somehow wise man, with a solitary but extraordinary view of life.

I published the piece in *Tracks* a month later and soon got a message from Dora through an intermediary, threatening to sue, castrate and torture me. Jack McCoy was pissed off too. 'I agreed not to interview him,' I protested. 'I didn't say I wouldn't write about our conversation.' The heat didn't last long, although Miki never forgot that I had 'exploited' him. I was on his burn list for twenty years.

In 1995 my wife and I started spending time each northern summer in the southwest of France, staying at the guest villa of our friends Harry and Sandee Hodge. These summer sojourns eventually turned into work projects, first the biography of surfer Jeff Hakman and, later, consulting work for Quiksilver Europe. Soon I was spending most of the year in France, living in a two-bedroom walk-up flat above the Tabac du Fronton in Guethary with a view over the left-hand break called Les Halcyons. In the flat directly below lived Miki Dora.

I can't remember spending much time with Miki before July 1998, when he was a fixture at the Quiksilver-sponsored Biarritz Surf Festival, pocketing the free hors d'oeuvres in the VIP tent. During the festival he was a guest of Harry and Sandee at a dinner party on the terrace of their hillside home. Miki was gregarious all night, swapping ribald stories with his old friend and business partner, the famous big-wave rider Greg Noll. At one point he sidled up to former world champion Midget Farrelly's wife Beverley and said, 'I don't believe I've had the pleasure.'

'Don't you remember me, Miki?' said Bev Farrelly. 'You tried to hit on me at Malibu in 1963.'

It was a great comeback and threw Miki completely. He made a stagy exit across the terrace with footwork reminiscent of Jerry Seinfeld's sidekick Kramer.

At the end of 1999 Miki Dora was part of a Quiksilver group invited to celebrate the new millennium in Fiji. It was a wonderful party that no one enjoyed more than Miki, except that as the dawn of the millennium approached, Miki grew more introspective. He confided in several people his absolute belief that the world would end at midnight. When it didn't, he still wasn't happy. We were on the edge of the planet here, he said. In New York and London the shit would hit the fan, computers blowing up, people rioting in the streets, cops and militia gunning them down like dogs. Chile would be the only safe place to be, he said.

And indeed, in the first week of 2000 he bade us farewell and lit out for Chile, not returning to France for several months.

One clear winter morning in February 2001, I sat drinking coffee with Miki at the *bar tabac* beneath our apartments. On a whim, I asked, 'How long since you were in Australia?'

'Too long,' he said. 'I kinda like that place.'

'Would you like to come out next month as the guest of a surf festival?'

'There'd have to be a contract,' he said. 'I'm not a frickin' sideshow.'

And so began one of the more interesting chapters of my intermittent personal association with Miki Dora. Since 1998 my wife and I, and our business partners, had been running the annual Noosa Festival of Surfing. Against all odds, we had managed to get the somewhat truculent Midget Farrelly to participate in a reenactment of the 1964 world championships final the previous year — but to land Miki

Dora as a guest . . . It would never happen, I was told over and over again. 'Oh, he'll take the ticket and the hotel room,' people said, 'but you'll never see him.'

Apart from a lifetime of such behaviour, the most telling evidence against Miki was his acceptance of an invitation to attend the Oxbow World Longboard Championships at Malibu a few years earlier. Oxbow got the bills, but they never saw Miki. However, since he'd mentioned it first, I drew up a contract which required his attendance at several social events during the course of the week-long festival, and stipulated exactly what we would pay for and what was to be Miki's responsibility. I should have known better.

I flew to Australia later that month and awaited the arrival of Dora and the dozen or so other surfing notables we had invited. Eventually I got a call from Brisbane Airport: 'Da Cat has landed.' The legends were ensconced at the South Pacific Resort, a couple of kilometres back from the surf but beautifully landscaped with cool poolside gardens and cabanas. Miki was apparently quite happy there, because we rarely saw him at the beach. But he did honour his social obligations. It was only on the who-pays-for-what that we ran into trouble.

One day, surfers Robert August, Mark Martinson and Wingnut Weaver asked Miki to make up a foursome for golf. Late in the afternoon I got a phone call from Wingnut at the country club. 'Miki says you're paying for him.'

'Jesus, Wingy . . . what are we talking about here? Fifty bucks? You pay and I'll fix you later.'

'Ah, it's actually a bit more than that.'

Miki, it transpired, had gone berserk in the pro shop and run up a very large bill, which he was insistent that I would pay. Faced with some bad PR we didn't need in a small resort town, I gave them a credit card number and bit my lip.

On the morning of Miki's departure, I had a call from the front desk of the South Pacific. 'Mr Dora is checking out and he refuses to pay his phone bill. He's getting very abusive.' I asked to speak to him.

'Come on, Miki, you know the deal. You've got the contract.'

'I haven't made any phone calls. They've got the wrong guy.'

I jumped in my car and drove to the resort, where Miki was pacing around the lobby, muttering at the staff and making theatrical gestures with his hands.

'Mr Dora,' said the duty manager, 'has made twenty-nine international phone calls and refuses to pay.'

Miki exploded. 'I never touched my room phone.'

'Mr Dora,' said the exasperated manager, 'every day you've come down here, asked us to get numbers for you, then spent hours talking to people on that phone there.'

'Oh, *that* phone,' said Miki, pointing to the lobby phone. 'That's not *my* phone.'

Of course, there was only one way out. Friends later said, almost admiringly, that Miki had got me on a technicality. But at the time I was furious. Miki needed a ride to the airport, where I too was bound. I fumed all the way, my wife and I in the front of the little RAV4, Miki in the back with our bags. He kept muttering about the 'public phone' in the lobby. I badly wanted to hit the bastard.

As it turned out, Miki and I were on the same flight to Singapore. I was on a Quiksilver-paid-for business class ticket. Miki was on the economy ticket I'd bought him. I knew this was going to be ugly.

'I'm with him,' he told the check-in clerk. 'We want to sit together.'

'I'm sorry sir, this is an economy ticket.'

'No, no — I'm with him, godammit!'

I made a hasty exit through the security gates while Miki hurled abuse over the counter. At Changi Airport I saw him in the transit area and took him to the Qantas Club Lounge, where he availed himself of the buffet bar and sat down opposite me on the comfortable chairs. Relaxed now, after a good sleep and a few glasses of wine, I suddenly saw the funny side of it all. I started laughing and Miki followed. Soon we were both cracking up.

As offensive and unfair as he could be, it was difficult to stay mad at Miki. Besides, the worse he stung you, the better the dinner party stories later on.

A couple of months after his return home from Australia, Miki had an annoying tumour on his neck removed and tests revealed that it was cancerous. Further tests showed that the cancer had spread to several organs. Miki took the news in typical fashion: it simply wasn't possible. He then decided to fight the disease his own way. Always a healthy, albeit eccentric eater, he stocked his flat with rice, vegetables and juices, plus vitamin supplements of all descriptions. Because his own kitchen was too small, he would brew up huge pots of healthy soup at Susan McNeill's Surf Hut restaurant and slip into the kitchen there to heat some up each evening.

He believed his other chance for survival was through complete relaxation, which he pursued by playing tennis and golf with his small circle of Guethary friends. But Miki's approach to both games was anything but relaxed. An atrocious loser, he once accused Australian surfboard shaper Phil Grace of arranging to have the bells of the Guethary church ring just as he was about to serve. People on adjacent courts who spoke above a whisper were abused until they shut up or left.

On 11 August 2001 a group of about twenty friends celebrated Miki's sixty-seventh birthday at the beautiful Chez Francois in the village of Biriatou, on the Spanish border. It was the kind of social event that Miki had pretended to loathe for much of his life, yet on this warm evening on the terrace overlooking the Bidassoa River, he played the tables like a politician, moving from one group to the next, full of smiles and funny stories. It was a particularly poignant occasion, because all of us there knew that for Miki there would not be many more.

A few days later I left for Ireland for a month, and when I returned on 10 September I was shocked to see how much Miki had aged. His weight was slipping away and he had developed a stoop. His spirit was still good ('Dead man still walkin'' was his cheerful hello) even when the catastrophic events of the next day in New York convinced him again that the world was about to self-destruct. In fact, in a strange way I think 9-11 made him more accepting of his illness. It reinforced his fatalism.

As the summer faded away, Miki kept on surfing as much as he could, although he no longer really had the strength to push himself on to the face at Guethary. I ran into him panting on the stairs one evening, dripping wet in the gloom, leaning on the stair-railing gasping for air. I asked if I could help. 'It's OK, I've got oxygen inside,' he said, nodding in the direction of his apartment. Oxygen. We were on the last straight now.

The morning I left Guethary to return to Australia for the southern summer, I slipped a note under Miki's door, telling him to contact me if there was anything he needed — like, say, Vegemite, 'that black shit'. I knew as I pushed the note under the door that it would be my last contact with Miki Dora.

A couple of weeks later he too left Guethary, returning to the care of his father and stepmother in Montecito, California, where he died peacefully just after New Year's.

In April 2002 Harry Hodge organised a memorial for Miki on the terrace overlooking Guethary. His father Miklos (a sprightly and dapper ninety-year-old) travelled from California and several of Miki's oldest friends came from around the world. Those who couldn't make it, like Greg Noll, sent written tributes. Local surfers Christophe Reinhardt and Francois Lartigau paddled Miki's ashes out to the break, the mayor of Guethary unveiled a memorial plaque, and we all went off and had a few drinks, a few tears and a lot of laughs.

Two days later I walked down to the terrace to check the surf and discovered that two of the screws holding Miki's plaque in place had been removed in an obvious attempt to convert the memorial to private memorabilia. I replaced the screws but within a week the plaque was gone. Ah, Miki, your memorial's a prized trophy on some shithead's wall. Exploited to the end.

First published, in part, in the *Surfers Path*, 2005.

20

PADDLE MADNESS

One man's true story of his and his little brother's attempt on the silver edition Molokai to Oahu Paddleboard Race

Nick Carroll

It was about four hours into the whole crazy bloody ultra marathon, and Oahu was finally beginning to loom up close enough for us to count the houses lining the cliffs behind Sandy Beach, when I stuck my right arm into a patch of unusually cool water and immediately knew we were in serious trouble.

'We're *fucked!*' I yelled, before a chunk of North Pacific came flying in from the right and slapped me silly for about the 540th time that day.

'What?' screeched Tom from the boat rail.

'We're' — slap! — 'fucked.'

'You've got another ten minutes!'

'Yeah, but —' Slap! Didn't the fool understand? Seven miles still to slug through before turning the corner for the last sprint to the finish line, and already we'd encountered The Current. The satanic Ka'iwi Channel current of island legend; the one that sucks along the eastern rim of Oahu and blows north like an express train, dragging anything mad enough to get trapped in it way the hell up to Kahuku, thirty nautical miles away. The Current that's supposed to be a mile or two wide — but today, of all days, had decided to fatten itself out by a multiple of five. And now, after twenty-five roaring, burning paddle-miles, we were expected to *cross* the fucker?

Ahh, what the hell, I thought. Let him find out for himself.

Allow me to explain something. Tom and I had absolutely no reason — on the surface of things — for putting ourselves through this blistering aquatic torture. Weren't no misplaced nostalgia, that's for sure. We're fully fledged hardcore modern waveriders, as likely to own a museum-style collection of 1950s redwood–balsa guns or a set of mint-condition 'Endless Summer' posters as we'd be to deliberately cut off most of our limbs. We're about as sentimental as a couple of woolly old tiger sharks. Our surfing language is fricken' digital, bro.

But in truth, the sheer inanity of modern professional surfing had finally begun to wear on us. Apart from anything else, it seemed now to be almost entirely divorced from the sport's core philosophy, the thing that'd fired every great surfing achievement of the last hundred years, from Duke Kahanamoku's resurrection to Mike Stewart's first big pits at Teahupo'o: the legendary tradition of the all-round Waterman — the surfer who, alone with his board, was at home in any ocean, anywhere. Once upon a time, for instance, the ocean paddleboard race was surfing's keynote competitive pastime; indeed, for many years prior to the Gidget Decade of the 1960s, a top surfer was in essence a Paddler. The challenge of paddle racing harked directly back to Duke's Olympic-swimmer background, to the classic Hawaiian inter-island canoeing tradition, and to the burgeoning lifeguard/lifesaver movements in California and Australia, where many surfers of the '30s and '40s found employment for their unique blend of water skills. Paddleboarding drove the great American surfer Tom Blake to reinvent the ancient board design of kings, the *olo*, during the '20s — chambering the board for reduced weight and eventually attaching the first ever surfboard fin. Blake forced other surfers to pay attention to his invention by destroying them horribly in paddle races, setting sprint times that paddlers were still striving to break thirty years later.

In 1953 Blake coached his protégé, California's Tommy Zahn, in a crossing of the Ka'iwi Channel, only the second time it'd been done on a paddleboard in modern history (the first was by Gene 'Tarzan' Smith in 1938). Zahn trained for months, paddling up and down Oahu's east side and finally doing the crossing one late October day with Blake watching from the rail of his escort boat. He made Diamond Head, a nice straight downwind run, in nine hours and twenty minutes. Three years later, Zahn's paddling skills took him to Australia for a lifeguard demonstration associated with Melbourne's 1956 Olympics, where he, Greg Noll and a couple of buddies introduced Australian surfers to balsa–fibreglass boards, laying the foundations for the next forty years of surfing progress.

By any standards it was grand, sweep-of-history stuff. High Macho, perhaps even High Camp when peered at in some lights, but real and raw enough to survive the planet's weirdest ever century. Yet in the face of this spectacular Olympian background, pro surfing — especially in the past five years or so — had shrivelled into a near parody of the Waterman ethic. Far from being the regal call-to-arms that core surfers have a right to expect from the sport's supposed Top Gun Academy, it was looking more and more like an obscure, juvenile crapshoot, a college for brilliantly talented rich kids constantly on the lookout for the Soft Option — to the point where many of the pros began to insist on being escorted out the back by jet ski, during major tournaments at places like Bells Beach in Australia, to spare their aching limbs the torment of a 200-metre paddle.

Towed *out*, for Christ's sake! Were these the depths to which Hawaii's sport of kings had sunk?

In any case, by the turn of 2001 Tom and I were restless, ready for some sort of new adventure to mark the new century, and the Silver Edition Molokai to Oahu Paddleboard Race — thirty-two straight-line miles of the world's most chaotic water — seemed to offer a chance of that . . . and a chance to pay some overdue respect to an era and a group of surfers worthy of the name. Partly it was the appeal of the complete unknown: was it even *possible* for a couple of witless surfers to paddle that far, that fast? Partly it was also pure ignorance of the torture involved in that vast grinding journey across the Ka'iwi Channel.

Of course, perhaps it was also a sign that three decades of saltwater had won out over our brain cells, and that we'd finally lost the freakin' plot.

Hawaii in the summer is a different place. The light is brighter and a little harsher. Driving across the fields above the North Shore, your view down to the ocean is not obscured by the big green sugarcane crops, because in July the cane is dead. Withered and dry, it lies half flat in golden yellow rows, the tradewind pinning it to the red earth. The water is clearer than the air, and sailboats anchor smugly in Waimea Bay, secure in the knowledge that no sensational bomber of a northwest swell is going to arrive overnight and blast 'em into atomic particles.

The Carroll brothers awoke blinking in the unaccustomed glare, surrounded by piles of giant slaughtered ants.

We'd flown in from the depths of a Sydney winter to a Honolulu midnight, and by 2am were rummaging around the back of our friend Hornbaker's North Shore hideout. 'Just break in,' Horny had assured us. 'I'll be there in a day or so. But I'm warning you, I don't know what it'll be like — I haven't been in there for three years.' The house was in fact full of ants — big, amiable Hawaiian sugar ants half the size of your thumb. The ants seemed a little stunned that human beings even existed, much less came crashing into their private universe and trying to lie down on the beds. They weren't stunned for long; fairly soon they were dead.

Like some stupid insects were gonna be able to resist *trained athletes*?

Oh, yeah! We'd trained! In fact, we started serious training for the race sometime in early April, with a bunch of paddle–swim sprint sets around a buoy anchored off our home beach, Newport, on Sydney's northside. Sure enough, out came all the vicious sibling rivalry that'd typified our dealings ever since little Tommy stole my tricycle off the back deck of the family home at the age of three.

At first I gave Tom such a severe thrashing around the buoy he was convinced I'd been taking Nandrolone or EPO. 'You're on the gear, aren't you?' he'd snap accusingly. 'Look at you! It's not natural!'

'Nonsense,' I mocked. 'You've *never* been able to swim. Remember at the swim school? You'd just flail like a lunatic and sink to the bottom. Want me to go easy on you? I can, you know, if you want.'

The buoy's name was Kylie, or at least that's what was painted on its outer rim. After a while, Kylie became known as 'that bitch', or just 'bitch'. Pre-training conversations might start with something like 'Three sets of the bitch?' or 'Let's do the bitch'. After about a month of the bitch, Tom was beginning to pick up the pace. He almost beat me in one swim leg. Of course, he was wearing flippers at the time.

After a couple of months we canned Kylie and started some longer paddles, cruising up or down the coast with the prevailing winds for six or eight or ten miles at a time — an hour or more of intense, tail-chasing effort, in and out of rips, the backwash off headlands bouncing us around like a couple of little boats in a storm. This gave us our first taste of 'running', the use of wind-waves to glide at speeds beyond those achieved by mere paddling, and it freaked us out. You could *surf* doing this! Maybe, thanks to all those years of wave riding closer to the beach, we had some sort of hidden advantage . . . but would it be enough?

This did not at any time confuse us as to our status in the paddleboarding community. Put simply, we were (and still are) complete Paddle Kooks. The art of paddleboarding survives in unique fashion within the surfing world's oldest and most respected homelands: in Australia as an offshoot of the surf lifesaving clubs' Iron Man competition circuit; in California as a cultish remnant of the great Santa Monica lifeguard scene, supported by the annual Catalina paddle race, the oldest continuous such race in the world. In Hawaii, it's a natural extension of the world's ultimate hardcore surf culture, a culture afflicted by a perverse coastal torment — for six months of the year it's smashed with the planet's best and most challenging surf, and for the other six months it's flat. F-L-A-T.

Like Dave Dailey, Dave Kalama's tall, mellow racing partner, told us: 'We paddle all the time, all summer long. Hell, man, what else is there to do?'

The top paddlers have been working on technique and equipment and psyche for years, sometimes generations. Aaron Napoleon, Hawaii's great hope for the race, grew up in a great Waterperson family: his dad Nappy was a top paddler in Tommy Zahn's day, and mum Alona was a great outrigger paddle racer. Sleek as a greyhound, Napoleon had some lethal backup in Dennis Pang, the renowned North Shore big-wave rider and surfboard shaper. Dennis had prepared the most gorgeous-looking craft for Aaron's shot at the title, a hollow superlight 18-footer. We surprised him one afternoon while he was tuning the rudder mechanism — a rotating skeg, controlled by the paddler's feet from the deck using a short fibreglass stick. 'You gotta get it just right,' he muttered, tightening the controls with aircraft engineer precision.

'Are you guys ready for this?' Dennis asked Tom. 'Ready as I'll ever be,' was the little bloke's brave response.

Dennis fixed us with the steely look of a man who'll turn and paddle for closeout set waves at Waimea. 'Paddle racing's all about technique, man. Get the technique right and you can beat anybody. I'm an OK paddler, but Aaron will get me every time these days because he has the technique down.'

Technique? What the hell was that?

The afternoon following the Great Sugar Ant Massacre, we went for a test paddle down the North Shore with some of the gnarly Aussie paddlers. Mick Dibetta, chief lifesaver at Burleigh Heads in Queensland, holds the race record, a phenomenal five hours 22 minutes 38 seconds, which he set in 1997. That record drags him back to Molokai each year. 'I dunno if I'll be the one to break it,' he said at the race press conference, 'but I do wanna be there when it gets broken.' At 5pm we met Mick and two other Aussies — tall rangy Jackson English from Avoca Beach, and Aaron Bitmead, a large quiet solid character who lifeguards with Dibetta — down at Sunset Point, paddled a half-mile or so out to the tradewind line, and ran down the four or five miles to Three Tables near Waimea Bay. The three of 'em had big 17-foot concave bottom boards designed by the legendary Australian shaper Dick Van Straalen, and they kicked our arses with such ludicrous ease I wondered if we should perhaps just get back on the plane and fuck off home to Newport Beach and forget we'd ever heard of the Silver Edition Molokai to Oahu Paddleboard Race. We weren't even remotely in the same league as these big strong bastards.

But then I recalled that being Stock Team paddlers, we weren't really in the same race. There are numerous divisions in the Molokai to Oahu, mostly based on age, but the most significant difference between racers is their choice of craft. Stock is anything up to 12 feet; unlimited is anything bigger, usually in the 16- to 18-foot range, which provides a hell of a lot more leverage against most kinds of water. In paddling, as in some other areas of life, length is an advantage.

And after all, despite our Complete Kook status, everyone was willing to help us out. This is one of the coolest things about the race — the sheer camaraderie among all involved. Race organiser Mike Takahashi spent patient hours outlining the race track and possible tactics we might use. Oahu's Greg 'Mighty'

Quinn, a Stock solo entrant, offered to take us for a run around
Koko Head, where racers theoretically first encounter land in the
race's dying stages. We met the Mighty Quinn at the actual
finish line, loaded our boards onto his car and roared off around
to Sandy Beach on the other side of Oahu's eastern peninsula.
'It's kinda choppy,' warned Greg, and by God it was — but it also
bore a strong resemblance to Sydney's windy reverberating
coastline. *Bring it on*, I thought as we bounced around Koko
Head on the wind-waves, buffeted by the trades. This was the
kind of shit we understood.

Another of the coolest things about the race is that it's a
don't-look-back kind of deal: you go to Molokai with nothing
you can't stick on an escort boat, and paddle off the island
without leaving a trace except maybe your footprints in the sand.

This naturally requires some planning, and the way in which it
occurs is classically Hawaiian — you put your faith in friends, cross
your fingers, and trust it'll all work out somehow. Jeff Johnson, the
great North Shore veteran Waterman, had promised us he'd hook
up a good escort. He put us in touch with the escort fleet boss, LJ
Benson, who in turn connected us with boat owner-driver Wendell
Suto. LJ told us we should send our racing board — a slick 12-foot
pintail made by California paddleboard designer Craig Lockwood
— over on a special boat he'd organised, equipped with cushioned
racks to withstand the bouncy crossing. 'Just drop it off at Ricky's
place,' he said, giving us an address in Honolulu.

Despite all the tourist gloss along the Waikiki fringe,
Honolulu is really a working port town, raffish, messy and cool

the way only a good Pacific port town can be, with side streets full of dubious-looking storage facilities and dusty half-finished industrial bays. 'Ricky's place' turned out to be one of these — a big steel enclosure with a painted sign, RICKY'S UPHOLSTERY, running above its double-garage entry.

I parked the car and Tom walked over to examine the scene. He came back convulsed with silent laughter. 'Fuck, mate, it's like something out of "Hawaii Five-O",' he whispered.

Unable to resist, I leaped out and strolled over. Ricky turned out to be a mellow gentleman of some fifty years. He was hanging out with a buddy in a small office area on one side of a big open space which was filled almost to capacity with old couches, chairs, bits and pieces of wooden framing, and rolled-up drapery. What little space was left was filled with a beautifully restored, freshly spray-painted US '60s muscle car.

'Pretty nice, guys,' I said, gazing approvingly at the vehicle.

'Well, we gotta put an engine in her now,' said Ricky's colleague. He ran a loving rag around the bonnet.

'So, er,' said Tom, feeling driven to change the subject, 'where should we put the board?'

'Just stick it over there,' said Ricky, waving at three or four other paddleboards that'd somehow been fitted into a corner near the office. 'We'll take care of it.'

Yeah, OK . . . we've only trained for four months and flown from Australia. With forty-eight hours to go before takeoff, *why not* just leave our key piece of gear in a Honolulu upholstery warehouse?

It seemed like madness. But, truth to tell, madness of one kind or another had lurked in the background of this Watermanly endeavour from the start. There's nothing normal about surfing: it's a dangerous, crazy, fucked-up sport, full of unstable bastards who've seen too much sea and sky to be trusted. But there's *really* nothing normal about paddleboarding. All those hours out there on the ocean, thrashing away, counting the strokes, lost in a haze of sweat, with nothing but the sound of water slapping the board's underside and the occasional whale or shark for company — at times, it really does feel like you're walking a little too close to sanity's edge for comfort. And if there's one lesson we'd carried over from surfing into this wacky new realm, it was this: when you're feeling mad, *go with it.*

'There's no stores where we're staying on Molokai,' Takahashi had warned. 'If you want breakfast on race day, you're gonna have to take it with you.' Armed with this information, we'd gone to a Costco warehouse store and bought up big — vast slabs of energy bars, thirty-two litres of bottled water, a vat or two of fruit juice — and left it at Ricky's Upholstery for Wendell to pick up the night before the race.

Suddenly, we were done. There was nothing more to do but get on the plane and head for Molokai.

Hornbaker came with us. Horny had finally made it back from a photo shoot he'd been doing on the Big Island with this ridiculously sexy French model named Julie, who took one look

at the piled sugar ant corpses and the two half-naked unshaven
Australians and quickly booked a flight back to Los Angeles.

'I'm looking forward to this,' Horny grinned, meaning the
race. 'Maybe I should bring my flippers. Just in case one of you
needs rescuing.'

The whole point of the last couple of days before the race is
drinking lots of water, huge pools of the stuff, and eating
disgusting, uninhibited amounts of food — the theory being that
by race day it's too late to pack in the liquids and calories you'll
be forced to draw on in the Fever of Battle. Therefore, the first
thing we did upon landing on Molokai at 7am on Race Eve was
to head for the nearest restaurant. We found it in Kaunakakai, a
small town in the middle of the island which almost fitted a
tourist brochure description of a Cute Island Village, except
nothing in Hawaii is really cute — it's beautiful, or it's bloody
dangerous, or it's just kinda hanging around, marking time.
Kaunakakai fitted into category three.

It did have a cool little breakfast place, where Tom instantly
sat down and ordered the most horrible meal I have ever seen him
consume: three hamburger patties, each topped by a runny fried
egg, the whole thing swamped with a couple of pints of grey-brown
gravy. 'What the hell are you doing?' I demanded, aghast.

'Just felt like a bit of protein,' he said primly.

Good God, this was my partner. We were going to die.

A tall man wearing an old North Shore Lifeguard hat came
over to watch the feast. This was Rick Williams, who guarded
Ehukai Beach Park, otherwise known as Pipe. Rick was a race

entrant in the solo division. 'Mind if I tag along with you guys?' he said.

No problem. At least he knew where we were supposed to be going.

It only took a few minutes for us to realise that Rick was very serious about this race — so serious, in fact, that he'd decided to eat nothing except *poi*. This is a paste-like substance made from ground-up taro root and water, the dietary opposite of Tom's hideous breakfast. It tastes exactly like raw mashed potato. 'Pure carbohydrate,' boasted Rick, hoisting a couple of two-pound sachets over his shoulder. 'I'm gonna suck this stuff down all the way back to Oahu!'

I began to feel better. Rick was obviously as fucked up as we were.

Rick guided us out to the west, across an extraordinary dry landscape. Windward Molokai is a green tropical paradise, but over here on the leeward side it looked like the NASA probe photos of Mars: all red dirt and black lava chunks, moulded into weird half-animal shapes. For a while the ocean lay hidden behind this spacy geography. Then the road snaked over a ridge and we pulled over to take in the view, and saw just what we had to deal with.

From up here the ocean looked gorgeous — light green close in to shore, falling to a deep, rich blue offshore, the trades spattering whitecaps way across the channel like daisies in a vast azure field. Far, far away on the other side of that field loomed Oahu: the big dark slab of cliff at Makapu'u, the sharp peak of

Koko Crater, the saddle and smaller blob of Koko Head, and way off in the distance, its dimensions meaningless as in some child's toy model, the celebrated postcard image of Diamond Head.

The Ka'iwi Channel awaited our pleasure.

'That's a . . . long . . . fuckin' . . . way,' breathed Tom.

'*Fuck* it!' I snarled back. 'It's a piece of cake! We're gonna break the record!'

'No, you are not,' said Hornbaker quietly. 'You're going to find out the true meaning of humpback.' We gazed at him uncomprehendingly. 'Well,' he continued, 'you don't think they call humpback whales humpbacks because they've got humps on their backs, do you? No! That's not it at all!' His voice rose slowly to a screech. 'They're called humpbacks because that's what they do. They *hump backs*! And tomorrow you're gonna be out there in the middle of the *ocean* and one of them is going to *leap* on you and . . .'

He waved his arms in a horrible pantomime of the seemingly certain inter-species buggering that awaited us mid-channel. Rick tried to back away, keeping his eyes fixed on Hornbaker. 'You know,' he said, 'if you go to the north side of the island, there's this big rock up there somewhere. It's round and tall and shaped kinda like a penis. They call it Dick Rock. Maybe you should go visit it.'

They were clearly affected by paddle madness. Ignoring them, staring at the channel instead, I began to see just how much a good tradewind could save your bacon in what lay ahead. The trades were pushing from the east-northeast, slightly across the race's line; yet even so, at 15 knots or stronger, they'd put enough bump on the channel to leave a solid paddler awash with runs — and during a run, you get to rest. Sort of.

We headed down to the coastline and the Kalua Koi Hotel, where everyone stays the night pre-racing. Or I should say the ex-hotel — its bankrupt owners had closed the hotel area, and the condos were suffering an invasion by eighty or so nervy, slightly manic paddlers, who by this time were lolling around on the lawns in front of the weirdly deserted complex.

It was great to see all our fellow psychotics gathered in one place. We were stunned to come across Dave Parmenter, the great surfer/shaper who now lives in Makaha; none of us had seen him in years. Parmenter was in excellent form, pondering Tarzan Smith's channel crossing in '38. 'No boat, nothing,' he muttered. 'No bottled water . . . you can just see him, grabbing seabirds out of the air and ripping their heads off and drinking their blood.'

Everybody kept saying, 'It's gonna be fun tomorrow!' This worried me more than almost anything so far on the trip. Would it be? Crazy, yeah — impossible, maybe — but *fun*?

Takahashi had told us we'd toss and turn all night out of nerves. I slept like a slaughtered sugar ant and woke at 5am, feeling sharp and rested. It was cool, even chilly, and the tradewind was still flapping the palms.

We'd been wondering what the hell Wendell Suto would be like in person. 'He's gonna be . . . big,' Hornbaker declared. 'A big Hawaiian. With enormous calves.' In fact, Wendell turned out to be a very cool-looking, suave, unflappable individual of relatively normal human dimensions, which were more than made up for by his friend Bob. Bob's calves were big enough for both him and Wendell.

Wendell brought the boat, a 6.6-metre open cabin Boston Whaler named *Hoku*, in near the shore, and Tom and Horny scrambled on board. Having volunteered for the first paddle set, I wandered around on the sand with the board, purposely averting my eyes from the daunting vision of far-off Oahu, now almost invisible behind a tradewind haze. Racers stood or sat alone or in their teams. Nobody was talking about fun anymore. They were shaking each other's hands and murmuring 'Good luck, bro', like Allied soldiers about to charge Omaha Beach.

With a few minutes to go, I paddled out near the starting line. All sorts of tricksy jostlings were going on — some paddlers deliberately heading up to the north buoy, some pegging out the south, a lot trying to shuffle into midfield, and a few blundering around not sure where they should go. Confidently, I sauntered up and parked right in the middle, sneering like I knew exactly what the fuck I was doing. Then someone in a boat just to the northwest blew a loud horn, someone else in the same boat waved a flag, and we were off.

I had this half-formed plan in mind to try to get us into the middle of the pack. Just as well I didn't plan to take the lead. Aaron Napoleon took off like he'd seen a tiger shark. He vanished off into the blue, spray flying everywhere while almost everyone else in the race sorta watched him go.

The first twenty minutes of a big paddle are some of the hardest. Your body is trying to squeeze blood through the muscles of your back and arms and get a clean flow of energy established. Your lungs are trying to suck oxygen and blow CO_2 at a new, grinding pace. Five or ten minutes into it, you're stiff as a board and feeling every stroke. Then, slowly, everything starts to smooth out; the muscles soften and stretch, the breathing settles into a rhythm, and you're gently hypnotised by the simple alternation of the stroke: one-two-one-two-one-two-one-two-one . . .

Your mind drifts away and cruises a bit above it all, making small decisions about pace and chop-runs, and watching the body almost incuriously as it begins to chew into its energy reserves. In a strange sort of way it's almost restful — unless your brother and your best mate are in a boat next to you, yelping, 'Smile! Smile for the camera!'

Paddlers spread out across the field, trying to draw one line or another toward the thin streak of land out beyond all that water.

Back on the boat, Wendell was revealing himself as a master strategist. 'We wanna go up, man,' he said as I crashed into the boat after the first half-hour set. 'Up and across the wind. Get dat wind in line with where we're going. Then turn down and run with it. All dose other guys, dey look like dey're in front . . . but eventually dey're gonna have to turn and come back in. It's pay now, or pay later.'

OK. Let's pay.

The half-hours ticked over. Well, they ticked over if you were in the boat. If it was your set on the board, they dragged out into a long welter of rhythmic charging sprints across the windline and deceptively difficult runs downwind, sharpened every few minutes by a glimpse of tiny Oahu or a yell — 'Eight minutes! Smile!' — from the boat. Between sets, downing another litre of water and trying to eat an energy bar, I watched my little brother admiringly. His stumpy arms were whirring away, his shoulders impregnable, his gaze focused forward into the task. All that training was really paying off. But then: oh, no! As the board lifted for another downhill run, something in me sensed a horrible change in the short, powerful frame — some ancient reflex calling to little Tommy's soul from a long-past, energised moment — and sure enough, with the board accelerating comfortably into its run and the need for power paddling briefly put aside, he cast away sense and intelligence and jumped to his feet.

Ten miles out, in the middle of the ocean, and Tom decides to go surfing . . .

'Paddle!' I screamed.

'Yeahhh!' Wendell screamed.

'Do it again,' Hornbaker screamed. 'I'll get my camera!'

'Yeahhh. Like Waimea Bay!'

'Again!'

'Like Pipeline!'

'Paddle!'

The energy bar stuck in my throat as I watched, waiting for the inevitable stumble, the ten pointless minutes that'd be spent retrieving the board, the lifetime of recriminations. Horny clicked away, Wendell grinned, Bob chortled, I pounded my head against the side of the cockpit.

In the end we were saved by a fish. A flying fish as big as a goddam kookaburra. It must've seen the short, terrible form of Carroll the Younger bearing down on it from the east, and panicked. The silvery beast sprang into the air and rocketed right across Tom's bows, eliciting a frightened screech from the former two-time world surfing champion. I knew exactly what he was thinking: The Humpback!

'OK, you guys,' declared Wendell in his best Hawaiian Waterman tone, 'time to go downwind. Time to make some ground, man!' Instantly we sobered up. No more tomfoolery. Let's just get through this.

You lose perspective out there in mid-channel. It's as if you slowly fall away into your own little hole in the ocean, your own strangely euphoric, endorphic world of pain. By now we were way upwind and out of range of almost all the other racers. Off to the south, a dozen or so boats stood out near the horizon; some were even tracking behind us. One was floating tantalisingly about half a mile in front, and one was hanging off to the north on a similar track. The tradewind was pushing at a consistent 10 knots, stronger in gusts, and windswell sets of four to six feet rose around us, a beautiful foam-flecked late morning blue.

We shortened the sets down to twenty minutes and I went out furiously hard, wanting to kill off the paddler to our north. It worked. By the time I flopped back into the boat, Oahu was visibly closer and the northerly boat had dropped off the pace.

But at what cost? For the first time in the race — for the first time since any of this whole paddle madness had started, months before — I felt sick and drained, shivering with exhaustion, coming to the end of my physical resources. Swallowing water was a serious effort, and a bite of a power bar nearly made me throw up. Out on the board, Tom looked like he was fighting the water, his arms rolling over slower and slower between runs. How long before they just stopped altogether? I tried to recall something Jamie Mitchell, a young race veteran from Queensland, had said the day before while we flopped around in front of the Kalua Koi. 'You'll hit a wall,' he warned. 'Round the twenty-mile mark. Team or solo, it won't matter. The thing is to just keep going, and you'll come out the other side.' As I jumped overboard for the next set, I clung to that thought like a straw in a whirlpool.

And the thing was, Jamie was right. Halfway into the set I began feeling an odd sensation — an unexpected freeing and loosening of the muscles, as if an old stiffened skin was burning, peeling away. I'm sure there's a valid biochemical explanation for this, some predictable bodily shift to a long-term energy source, but out in that channel, focusing on run after run, sickness receding and fresh heart pouring in to take its place, I got the distinct impression that I was being literally reborn.

Of course, about then the water turned cooler all of a sudden, the telltale ribbing of a riptide flickered across the downwind line, and I suddenly realised ... Oh, crap! This is where the race *begins*.

Perhaps I'll spare you the rest of this horrendous tale: the crabwise crawl across the mighty current; the Viking-like lust overcoming us upon reaching Koko Head; the five-minute sprint sets to the finish line; the last-minute death battles with fellow paddlers. The boat that'd tantalised us from a half mile in front turned out to be Mighty Quinn's. We caught and passed him just at the final turn toward home: 'I'm never doing this race again,' he muttered.

French people call orgasm the Little Death. Well, in my opinion, getting to the end of the Silver Edition Molokai to Oahu Paddleboard Race is way too close to the Big Death. Past the finish line you come into a tiny bay, where a very nice man gives you a bottle of water and offers to carry your board up onto the grassy verge. Slumped against a tree and temporarily speechless, I watched people homing in on the finish. Paddlers arrived on Oahu in one of two states: either hyped on adrenalin or almost unable to walk. Everyone had a story, but most were just too buggered to tell it. Eleven paddlers pulled out during the race, among them Aaron Napoleon. His early pace had left him shattered by cramps on the rim of The Current — that, and by the relentlessness of the other Aaron, Bitmead. Takahashi, who'd watched the whole drama from the official boat, told me the young Aussie lifesaver never let Napoleon out of his sight and eventually hit the front about two and a half hours into the race. 'It was one of the best demonstrations of wave riding that I have ever seen,' was Mike's call.

Aaron didn't say much — just lay around under one of the tent-shades that'd been set up at the finish, and ate a very large plate of spaghetti. He won $1500, which might just have paid his travel costs. (Nobody actually makes money doing this! Making money is a pursuit of sane people, not mad ones.)

Hornbaker thought it was all too funny for words. 'You'll never know how near that humpback came,' he said grimly. Tom seemed to spend a lot of time in the toilet; I doubt he'll be eating hamburgers with eggs and gravy for breakfast again for a while, or energy bars, for that matter.

As for me . . . well, just before the race, I worked out in my head that I'd given up 200 surfing hours training for the Molokai to Oahu . . . and now it's over, I'm gonna go get 'em back.

First published in *Big* magazine, 2001.

21

LEAPER

If you turn to the ocean for sanctuary, you might be looking in the wrong place

Tim Winton

Leaper drove the van along the hard sand and saw the signs of a good swell. Where the beach ended in a sand-spit point he parked and got out. It was still early morning. A long drive from the city. The hot easterly rushed across the sand onto the water and out on the reefs it tore the tops from clean-breaking waves. He chucked off his clothes and pulled on a pair of shorts. From the roof he took his surfboard. He waxed it and, down at the water's edge, strapped on the legrope.

Inside the reef the water was calm. Between the reef and the beach was a small island whose limestone jags were blotched with guano. It was a good kilometre out to where the swells rose on the reef and peeled off, hollow and long. As he paddled, keeping rhythm with a song in his head, Leaper looked down at the wavering coral-flecks on the limestone lumps below. Maybe later he would snorkel for some fish. It would make the day complete, and with that sense of completion he would gird himself for the trip home to the housework and the baby, to his silence.

When he got near the break, Leaper was surprised to see another surfer drop down the face of a big, grinding right-hander. For a few moments the figure was lost in the churning guts of the wave. Leaper sat up. The wave spat the rider onto its shoulder with a rush of trapped wind. Bearded, heavy, tanned, the man slewed over the back of the wave and settled in the deep water behind.

Leaper paddled up. 'Nice wave.'

'Plenty of 'em today.'

'Been out long?'

'Since dawn. It's a homewrecker, the sea.'

Leaper looked aslant at him.

'Quick.' The other rider pointed seaward. 'Out the back.'

Together they paddled hard to meet the rearing, feathered swells. Everywhere was spray and sunlight and upreaching force. Leaper and his companion scrambled atop the first and skittered down its back into the path of the next, leaving behind the sound of an avalanche. Leaper strained. It was exhilarating to feel small and anonymous. It was like being sixteen again, another chiacking schoolkid.

Out beyond the sneaking set, Leaper and the other surfer turned their legs in the pellucid water and caught their breath. Leaper saw the sheen on their skins and caught himself before that dormant part of him could store it and play with its possibilities. Sun on water, that's all, he told himself.

The other rider was big and going to fat, as old as Leaper, though perhaps older. Early thirties. Neither of them were kids anymore and it felt odd, the two of them out there. Like two old hippies, he thought. Still it wasn't as unpleasant as sharing the break with some nineteen-year-old hotshot with a Gestapo haircut and luminescent wetsuit.

'Your face is familiar,' the stranger said. He blew water and snot from a nostril with a thumb over the other. 'Seen you somewhere.'

Leaper shrugged. Supermarket? Petrol station?

'Surf here much?' Leaper asked by way of a diversion.

'Every day there's swell. Work as a deckie on a crayboat up here. Do some shearing after the season. Pick some fruit. Got a caravan in the park back there.' He pointed across the bay to where crayboats were moored near a jetty and radio masts stood above the squat bungalows of fishermen and weekenders.

'Must be ideal.'

'I got three kids and a wife. Cartin' 'em round in a van place to place. Hardly ideal. Took up surfing again to save meself from the bottle. And the wife's onto me about havin' a bloody stroke.' He held a roll of fat in his fingers. Leaper envied him.

Another set soldiered in toward them. Leaper positioned himself, dug hard, and got onto the first of them. He surged down the face; it was like flying. And that rush as he carved out wide and traced his hand on the face pulling back and tucking down for a long run across the winding wall — it was the same fresh excitement from his teens.

Leaper was glad he'd come back to surfing after all these years. Things like that had gone from his life as soon as he was caught up in his work, and there was less time still after his work became more than what he did alone during the day out of a compulsion and love for it. Surfing was one thing in his life that hadn't come easy to him. He was unexceptional at it; and since his retirement, it suited his craving for mediocrity.

Paddling back to the break, he saw the deckhand pass high on the shoulder of an incoming wave. The man spread fans of water with heavy, desperate turns. Funny, thought Leaper; he looks like he's trying to win something, like he's surfing for his life. Leaper did not think of that earnest face and canvas and oil and light. He put his head down and paddled. He felt the muscle-ropes tighten in his back.

Before long the surfer joined him in the lull between sets. The easterly began to ease. It was hot out on the water. Leaper saw glistening spots in the other man's beard.

'How long'll you keep it up? Working on the boats.'

The other man grinned. 'I got the sack this morning.'

'Ah.'

'Bad seas, bad boat.' He let off a short burst of laughter. 'Bad bloody luck.'

'Well, there's the dole.' The Bob Hawke Surf Team, they called it these days.

The man looked Leaper full in the face. He seemed suddenly much closer. Yes, Leaper thought; that's definitely a look of disbelief.

They rose and fell with the summer sun on their backs. Leaper felt the guilt again. Things had always fallen into place for Leaper. He'd worked hard and long, but sometimes his good fortune had felt indecent.

'I know who you are,' the surfer said, turning for the next wave. 'You're Leaper.'

The dimpled wall rose and took him with it and left Leaper behind in the spray. There he was again, accused of being Leaper. Happy Home Leaper. Promising Student Leaper. Gifted Artist Leaper. Early Success Leaper. Even in silence and retreat he prospered. He thought about turning around and paddling in right then. Back to the city. Reclaim the kid from the babysitter. Lock himself in his own house behind the hedges. Scrub shit off the toilet. Hang out some washing, be Leaper Househusband. But he waited for the other surfer.

'We studied at the same uni, same bloody department.'

Leaper stared.

'Fine Arts. FARTZ. I was gone before you got there. The year before. You were their star I heard.'

'Then how come —'

'I'm here? Wasn't any good mate. Competent, I s'pose. I could decorate Kentucky Fried Chicken boxes. But the real stuff?' He shook water from his beard. 'Anyway I married early. When I was studying. The kids came all in a rush. Bit of a disaster. I got out.'

'Shame,' said Leaper. He turned his hands in the water.

'Oh, I get the gear out now and then, you know, have a bash. Done a few oils of this place. Would've done 'em in watercolour but the kids use 'em all the time. They're dud paintings but the wife likes 'em. She's loyal.' He chuckled. 'I read somewhere that you retired.'

Leaper felt his eyes moving up the beach to where children's bicycles had left cross-hatching in the hard sand and a faint smear of weed met the water's edge. He saw it clear from afar.

'Yeah. I didn't have anything left to say.' What a farce, he thought; two retired painters gone surfin'.

'What, at twenty-six?'

'Twenty-eight.'

The other man cleared his nose. 'Chrissake.'

Leaper felt anger rise. 'There was nothing I could say. I stopped.'

'*Nothing?*'

A mob of gulls clattered past overhead and settled on the jagged upreaches of the island inshore.

'I drive a hundred miles for a surf and I get lectured about the processes of the creative mind by someone . . .' Leaper caught himself.

The other man smiled. 'You're a fucking snob.'

Leaper could have got off his board that moment and got him by the throat.

'For Chrissake, I'm the opposite. That's why I quit. Privilege. Look, mate,' he burst out, suddenly letting go a secret he swore he'd never let out. 'I quit because I felt guilty scrambling up over the backs of the mediocre, no matter how willing they were. There's a whole breed of artists who'll never make it, and the biggest pleasure you can give them is to climb over them, accept their help, their flattery, use their connections so they can feel close to the action, get some vicarious thrill from seeing you succeed. I didn't want that on my conscience any longer.'

'But didn't you want to be a painter? God knows I did.'

'Yes, but I just wanted to paint. I wanted it to be just.'

The other man cleared his nose again and smiled. Leaper thought he saw him mouth the word 'just'.

'Here am I,' the surfer said, incredulous, 'knowing that I can't do it, and you know you can and you just stop.'

'No, I'm like you, I can't.'

The other man looked hard at him. 'I've seen your stuff, mate. Say you don't want to if you like, but don't have the arrogance to say you can't. You're *not* like me. You don't know what it's like to be me.'

'And you think you know what it's like to be me?' Leaper had never been so angry.

The surfer looked sideways at him. 'I know what it *means* to be you. Having choices. Jesus Christ, and they call you a realist.'

Leaper sat rigid and saw a set looming. It took will to break free from himself and paddle. He dug his way onto a twisting left-hander. He rode hard and angry, pushing the board all over the wave, scoring it, taking risks, until he pulled out, gasping, and found himself knee high on the kelpy limestone reef. That sideways glance. He'd got it from his wife lately. Nothing spoken, only that look.

Joining the other surfer again at the break, Leaper said nothing. There was a tension between them. They sat with it tug-o-warring between them for a while. I don't want to be this different, Leaper thought. Why the hell must someone get the breaks at someone else's expense? He had to show him.

'What's your wife's name?' Leaper asked.

'Raelene. She's a good woman. Why don't you come back to the van later for a cuppa. She'd love to meet the real thing.'

Let it ride, Leaper thought; he's not being bitter. 'You told her about the job yet?'

He shook his head. 'Been out here since dawn, since the boat got back. We were saving for a deposit on a house. No, she doesn't know yet. Every man's a coward, eh?'

The sun was beginning to burn Leaper's back. It was time to go in. He turned to speak but there was the sudden sound of spray and a cross-surge of water. Leaper saw his companion lurch and scream. The man was jerked sideways along the water. He rolled, still astride his board, and Leaper saw the sweeping cut of the tail. Bronze whaler. Big. Leaper sat still. Pulse in his ears. The water boiled and the man's big body shook. Leaper saw the shadow in the water. And then it veered away and was out of sight. A pink smear spread on the water. It was a beautiful, incongruous colour. Leaper did not move. My God, he thought; my good God.

When the screaming man surfaced, Leaper discovered himself moving. Thirty metres away, moving seaward, a piece of surfboard bounced and skittered on the surface. Playing with it. Leaper paddled across and took the man by the hair. He began to tow him. The big man began to flail. The water churned with pillars of blood. Leaper made himself get off his board and into the swirling wash. The other man still held onto the remaining piece of his board. Leaper reached for him. Something brushed against his skin. He shrieked. He kicked at it. It touched him again on the knee and he saw how blue was the sky. He began to lash out indiscriminately. Once, twice, he hit something firm, and then he felt the length of it upward along his body. Five toes brushed across his navel. He heard himself shouting. He took it. He took hold of it. He hoisted it out of the water and onto his own board, foot, ankle, shin — a leg.

'Get over!' he shouted. 'Get on my board for Chrissake!' He pulled at the man's hair and struck him and shouted.

The man lifted his head and looked whitefaced at him. 'Shit and fucking corruption, I'm gonna die.'

Leaper got him onto his board in the end. The man slid on, right across his own leg, and began to sob. From behind, Leaper saw the ragged knee and the jets of blood. He tore the legrope off the remaining ankle and, treading water desperately, gulping and gasping, he tied the polyurethane cord around the flesh behind the stump. It seemed to stop the jets but not the seeping. The man trembled. Leaper held him by his good leg and began to kick. He tried frogkick, patterkick, scissorkick, but none seemed better than the others. He caught an eyeful of blood. The legrope was slipping; it wouldn't hold. Leaper aimed for the channel inside the island. Caravan full of kids, bad paintings, loyal wife, house deposit. Leaper's mind lurched all over.

He did not see the first wave of the set. From behind it reared, took them up and tossed them forward. There was no time to steer or get out. It was like falling from a tree. The bottom was hard and angled. It knocked the wind from him as he rolled across the reef. The weight of worlds was on him. He began to fight up.

When he surfaced, the board popped up beside him but that was all. He swivelled about. Across the exposed section of reef toward the island, the other man's board tumbled and stuck. Another wave bore down and he dived. Tumbling across the reef he thought to himself *I can't, I won't save him, I'm not capable* and when he found the surface again there was nothing but more waves and more battering, more reef and more and more of more until all he felt was his board racking his leg at the end of its tether.

In the shallows in the lee of the island, Leaper began to heave. It felt as though the pummelling and the sobs and the retching wouldn't stop until everything was dragged from him and his heart would halt, but when stillness came to him he lay with his head on the board. He felt sand between his fingers. It was a long time before he looked up. The shallows were thick with whitebait. The beach was still a good two hundred metres away. He saw sand cusps, light on the water. He saw a caravan — no, it was inside him. *Privilege, Leaper; the ultimate privilege. He's dead, you're alive. What'll you do, pretend you aren't?* There was no more room in him for silence, fake or real. He was Leaper and there was a scream coming up from inside him — colour, words, energy — and he wasn't going to stop it coming till the privilege of breath or body or brilliance left him. He opened his mouth and he knew the whole bay, the whole world, would hear him.

First published in *Tracks* magazine, 1987.

Glossary

Mark Warren

amp Get excited i.e. I'm amped to get out there.

backdoor An expression used to describe a situation where a surfer is forced to pull into an already pitching barrel from behind the peak.

banks Sand banks — the bottom contours formed by shifting sand that influence the shape of a wave.

barrel A term used to describe the breaking motion of a perfect wave. Same as pipe (1960s) and tube (1970s).

beachies Beachbreaks, waves that break over a sand bottom.

boardies Boardshorts or surfing trunks.

bodyboard Soft, flexible bellyboard, which can be used in flagged areas.

bomb A bigger wave, usually an unexpected big set or single wave 'out of the blue'.

bommie Abbreviation of bombora. A 'cloud break' or isolated, submerged offshore reef, where big waves break on large swells.

caught inside When a wave breaks outside a surfer paddling out, one of the worst situations to confront a surfer.

channels/channel bottom Ridges that run along the bottom of a surfboard, lovers of this design say it enhances speed and control.

choppy A term used to describe a certain condition of water surface, usually in strong onshore winds.

closeout Not nice. Caused by formless bottom profile, which creates a wave breaking simultaneously across an unmakeable width.

cloudbreak Famous wave in Fiji, also any outer reef that breaks in open ocean, i.e. breaking waves look like clouds on the horizon.

clubbies Volunteer surf life saving club members, once the avowed enemies of surfers.

cranking Optimum surf conditions. When the surf's goin' off, it's cranking.

ding Damage to the external skin of the surfboard.

dredging As strong waves break in shallow water they draw water from ahead of them, sucking already shallow water up into the face of the wave. A dredging wave is the big brother of a 'sucky' wave.

drop in Surfing's most offensive behaviour. To paddle and then drop in on a wave someone else is already up and riding, on the inside.

earlies/early session Going for a surf at dawn.

feral An unkempt, hippy-like character, sometimes travelling cheap to remote destinations.

filthy Same as hot, great, unreal, off-its-tits.

fins Small rudder like protrusions on the bottom of a surfboard to give it direction.

floater Has nothing to do with beer or pies. A floater is a new move, originated by the late Mark Sainsbury, where the surfer rides over the falling curtain of a breaking wave.

foamball Churning mass of foam inside the tube of the wave.

glassy When there is no wind, usually early in the morning when the ocean surface is silky smooth.

gnarly A dramatic term used to describe a wave with a real mean streak.

Goat-boater A surf ski rider. Definitely the most unpopular craft in the surf. Reputation for being greedy and aggressive in the water has lasted decades. They look like a big surfboard with a bulbous rear end, where the rider sits up and propels the surf ski with a double bladed paddle.

goin' off Also goin' mad. Ripping! Unreal! Happening! When someone is ripping in perfect surf.

goofyfoot One of the oldest terms still current in surfing jargon. Someone who stands on the surfboard with their right foot forward. Has nothing to do with being left- or right-handed.

grommet Same as gremmie (1960s). Young surfer, intent on maximising beach and in-the-tube experiences. Trainee surf mongrel on the way to full 'surf nazi' status.

groundswell A strong, long distance swell generated by a storm or weather system far from the coast.

gun A big wave surfboard.

gutsliders As above.

hold-down Can refer to an amorous lover, but more often relates to the way certain waves hold you down when you're caught in the whitewater, either after a wipeout or being caught inside.

Huey Mythical God of the surf.

inside Refers to area inside breaking waves, as in being caught inside by a big set. Can also refer to the barrel, as in 'inside the barrel'.

jacking The process by which a wave gathers water and elevates as it moves suddenly from deep into shallow water.

Jaws Big wave spot on the Hawaiian island of Maui, focus of tow-in surfing pioneers.

Kahuna Hawaiian wise men or priests, said to be able to bring up the surf.

kook A learner surfer, or beginner, one who shows poor ability.

ledges When an incoming swell meets underwater ledges of rock, usually reefs, the wave jacks up quickly and pitches forward in a powerful, thick lip.

left-hander A wave which breaks from right to left, looking at the beach.

lidders Bodyboard riders.

lineup The area in which surfable waves break at a particular spot.

lip The leading edge of a clean-breaking wave.

local Anyone who's been there a day longer than you.

longboard Traditional '60s style surfboard, generally over nine feet in length.

Malibu Also called 'mals' and longboards, these boards are over 2.4 metres (8 feet) and similar to boards of the 1960s. Specially suited to older, physically impaired people or young mental retards.

Mavz/Mavericks Big wave spot in Northern California, renowned for big, cold, dangerous surf.

max-out Over the limit, over the top, exaggerated expression as in 'the huge swell maxed out!' Also used to define upper limit of a particular wave, as in 'this wave maxes out at two metres'.

mushburger A shapeless wave, caused by unfavourable winds. Some spots just don't have a good bottom contour and the waves are always mushburgers.

natural-foot A surfer who stands with left foot forward.

noah Rhyming slang, as in Noah's ark = shark, the animal all surfers dread. Varieties include bronzies (bronze whalers), formula ones (hammerheads), terries (tiger sharks) and the surfer's favourite, the white pointer.

nor'easter The prevailing summer winds along Australia's east coast.

North Shore Of Oahu, the most famed surfing coastline in the world.

NSSA The USA's National School Surfing Association

offshore When the wind blows from the land out to sea; the best wind for quality waves.

oil/oily Exceptionally smooth, glassy surf, usually associated with no wind.

onshore When the wind is from behind the waves.

outside When you're out in the water and someone yells 'Outside!', it usually means there's a big set approaching the break.

peak That part of the wave which breaks first over the shallowest section of an undulating bottom.

pintail A narrow, pointed tail on a surfboard.

pipe/Pipeline Famous wave in Hawaii, extremely hollow, critical and dangerous, breaking over shallow lava reef.

pitching A term used to describe the way the top part of a wave elevates (jacks up) and throws forward. This is caused by the wave suddenly moving from deep into shallow water.

planshape The shape of the outline of a surfboard.

quiver A collection of surfboards owned by one surfer.

rail The edge of a surfboard.

reform Often waves break on an outer sandbank or reef, before moving across deep water and then reforming, usually as a shorebreak.

right-hander A wave which breaks from left to right.

shacked Nineties expression for tubed or barrelled extra-deep.

shaper One who shapes surfboards.

shorebreak Waves that break directly on to the beach, usually in a dumping action.

shortboard The most popular modern equipment, around six feet, generally for small waves.

sick When the surf's so good it's beyond excellent, it's sick.

sketchy Dangerous, or shady. Risky.

sloppy With an onshore wind, waves collapse, shape is formless, and it's sloppy.

snaked Cheated out of a wave by a bit of sneaky positioning.

soul surfer One who surfs purely for love, not fame or money.

square An expression used to describe an extremely hollow wave, on which the bottom drops quickly as the top pitches, stretching the wave face vertically, creating 'corners' on the wave profile. Dangerous.

stand up The motion of a swell as it comes out of deep water and rises to break.

stroked Paddled.

sucky Like dredging only slightly less awesome.

surf overhead To surf waves that are over head height, i.e. bigger than six feet.

top-to-bottom Two possible meanings: 1. a very thick, hollow wave — a top-to-bottom barrel; 2. a state of optimum ski cover at Thredbo.

tow-in Pulling a surfer into a wave using a tow rope and a jet ski.

waterman This expression started in the 1960s to describe a dedicated surfer who could also paddle a canoe, free-dive, swim like a fish and show tremendous endurance in any ocean situation. An all-round ocean athlete.

WCT (World Championship Tour) Pro surfing's most elite level of competition, that decides the world title.

wedgy A term used to describe how a swell refracts or breaks up, then stands up over a shallow bottom in a compact, peaky fashion.

white The most feared species of shark, the great white is common in colder waters off southern Australia.

whitewater The broken part of the wave, aka, foam.

wicked When the surf's goin' off or cranking (optimum conditions), it's wicked.

WQS (World Qualifying Series) As the name suggests, the tour you have to qualify through to get to the WCT.

About the Authors

Pam Burridge

Pam Burridge grew up in the Sydney harbour suburb of Clontarf and, after starting surfing on a backyard special at age ten, was a regular at Freshwater and Manly beach. She began surfing competitively at age twelve and went on to win many junior events, occasionally placing highly against the boys. In 1990 Pam won a much fought for World Title after ten years on the professional tour. Pam retired from competition in 1998 and has had two children, Isobel and Otis with her husband, surfboard shaper and former longboard champion Mark Rabbidge. They live near Bendalong on the South Coast of NSW. Pam still surfs regularly and runs surf coaching for beginners and up-and-coming surfers.

Fiona Capp

Fiona Capp is the author of *Writers Defiled: Security Service Surveillance of Australian Authors and Intellectuals, 1920 – 1960*; a memoir, *That Oceanic Feeling*; and two novels, *Night Surfing* and *Last of the Sane Days*. She lives in Melbourne but heads down the coast whenever she can, surfing mainly at Portsea on the Mornington Peninsula.

Nick Carroll

Nick Carroll has been writing about surfing almost ever since he learned to stand up on a surfboard at Newport Beach, Sydney, thirty-four years ago. Since then, aside from winning national surfing titles and riding waves on almost all the world's surfable coastlines, he's become the world's best known surf journalist. Nick has edited several major surf magazines, including *Tracks* and *Deep* magazines in Australia and *Surfing* magazine in California, where he lived for several years in the 1990s. He currently lives in Sydney, writing for and consulting with a wide range of publications worldwide, and surfing way too much. He is 46 and married with two children.

Sean Doherty

Sean Doherty is a freelance writer and has been the editor of *Tracks* surfing magazine for five years. He contributes to several magazines and newspapers worldwide, including *Surfer*, *Surfing*, *Trip Surf*, *Carve*, *Zig Zag*, *The Insider* and the *Sydney Morning Herald*. He has also written one book: *MP, The Life Of Michael Peterson*. He is a natural-footer whose surfing style has been described by some less than kind sources as being similar to Tarzan swinging through the trees. He lives a stone's throw from Dee Why Point in Sydney, where he can be found fading grommets onto the rocks and occasionally – very occasionally – getting barrelled.

Jack Finlay

Jack Finlay is sixty-one, and has been surfing, sailing, and diving, for most of his life. His articles and short stories have appeared extensively over a lengthy period of time in Australian, American, and European surfing, and yachting magazines. He is also the author of three books, *Bass Strait and Beyond*, *Caught Inside*, and *Fighters: 25 Australian Lives In and Out of the Ring*. Jack has been a member of Victorian surfing teams, is a former Victorian Veteran's Champion, and still an active surfer. For six years he was the inaugural manager of the Surfworld Surfing Museum. He lives in Torquay, Victoria, with his wife.

DC Green

DC Green is an award-winning fiction and non-fiction writer who has roamed the world for a variety of surf magazines (mainly because he couldn't afford his own air tickets). His first article for a surf magazine (*Tracks*) was published when he was just seventeen. 'Lash Clone', a twisted tale about a surfer from the planet Vortex, spawned over eighty episodes and a cult classic book. DC has since written a few thousand articles for over forty magazines, contributed to a dozen anthologies and just had his first novel for children published, *Erasmus James and the Galactic ZAPP Machine*. DC lives where he grew up, deep on the NSW South Coast. He continues to surf with high zeal and low skill.

Matt Griggs

Matt Griggs was born in 1976. Growing up in the beachside suburb of Cronulla in the south of Sydney, Griggs was raised in a beach-loving family alongside sporty brothers, a PE-teaching father and an ever-supportive mother. Sport consumed his life, but it was surfing that swallowed him whole. Griggs reached the top ten of Australia in the junior and open ranks, competing around the world as a professional surfer for six years. He retired in 1999 to work for *Tracks* magazine as a full-time writer for three years and is currently working for Ripcurl as Global Team Pitt Boss managing and coaching Ripcurl's World Championship Tour team.

Phil Jarratt

Phil Jarratt is a surf industry and surf publishing veteran. A former editor of *Tracks*, he is also the author of seventeen books, including the best-selling *Mr Sunset: the Jeff Hakman Story*. After five years based in France as head of Quiksilver Europe's marketing, he now resides in southern California while he writes a history of Quiksilver.

Andrew Kidman

Andrew Kidman is a writer/musician/filmmaker and surfer. Kidman has been writing for surfing publications since the age of fifteen, and was made editor of *Waves* surfing magazine when he was eighteen: a position he held for six years. In 1995, along with the Val Dusty Experiment he released the groundbreaking surfing film *Litmus*. In 1994 through Consafos Press in the US his children's surfing book *Way of The Bird* was published. In the same year he released his second surfing film *Glass Love* and his fourth album as the soundtrack to the film. He lives in the hinterlands of northern New South Wales with his daughter Bella Love and partner Michele.

Jimmy O'Keefe

The dullest of six kids, Jimmy O'Keefe grew up in Brisbane. He stole money and hitched rides to the nearest breaking waves with a board he also stole. He now pays dearly for his errant youthful crime sprees with his lot as a lowly paid journalist. After accidentally writing a History of Australian Surfing for the University of Queensland, parallel to a journalism degree; he soon became a feature writer at the *Australian Surfer's Journal,* and his blinding prose has since blessed every surf publication in Christendom. Jimmy is currently the editor of *Australia's Surfing Life* magazine.

Mark Warren

Mark was Australian Open Champion in 1976 just as the fledgling professional circuit was evolving. In the same year he won the prestigious Smirnoff World Pro at Sunset Beach in Hawaii. He went on to finish in the top ten of the world ratings for several years but retired after winning the Duke Kahanamoku Invitational at Waimea Bay in Hawaii in 1980. Mark has since worked as a commentator/host on Channel 9's Wide World Of Sports and the Triple M radio network and has written the *Atlas Of Australian Surfing* (HarperCollins, 1988). Mark now works for Quiksilver International but travels to popular surfing destinations worldwide and remains a dedicated and active surfer.

Tim Winton

Tim Winton was born in Perth. He has published nineteen books for adults and children, which have been acclaimed both in Australia and abroad. Three-times winner of the Miles Franklin Award, and shortlisted twice for the Booker Prize, his work has been translated into sixteen languages and has been adapted for stage, radio and film. He lives in Western Australia with his wife and three children.

Acknowledgments

I'd like to take this opportunity to thank all the authors who contributed to this collection, pulled together in some haste and with their great and swift co-operation. There were also plenty of worthy omissions, too numerous to mention, but hopefully this may be the first of many such collections.

I owe a great deal of gratitude to Geoff Carter at www.surfresearch.com.au for his assistance with many of the historical references in the introduction. His website is a treasure trove of such information. I also owe much to an amazing little publication, *200 Years of Surfing Literature: an annotated bibliography*. This incredible gem for any surf historian was published by Timothy T. DeLaVega (based on Daved Marsh's *The Water Log*), with funding from the Surfing Heritage Foundation in the USA. It lists virtually every surfing publication ever produced anywhere in the English-speaking world. Visit www.surflit.com for more information.

Thanks also to Jennifer Blau at HarperCollins for her patient and sensitive editing and understanding, and Alison Urquhart for the enthusiastic impetus to get this thing going in the first place. Also, thanks to Mark Warren for updating the glossary, originally gleaned from his excellent *Atlas of Australian Surfing*.

Special thanks to Jenny Darling and Associates and Tim Winton for permission to reprint 'Leaper', from the pages of *Tracks* magazine.

I remain grateful to all the talented, hardworking and long-suffering surf photographers who contributed their images, and who have sustained the magic and allure of surfing magazines for years far more effectively than mere words. And to the remarkably tolerant surf publishers who have given me employment over the last twenty years.

Finally, thanks to all those surfers who surf writers pester for a glimpse of their inner worlds, when they'd probably much rather be riding waves.

Tim Baker